the series on school re

Patricia A. Wasley	**Ann Lieberman**	
University of Washington	NCREST	New York University

SERIES EDITORS

(Continued)

This series also incorporates earlier titles in the Professional Development and Practice Series

THE COMPETENT CLASSROOM

Aligning High School Curriculum, Standards, and Assessment— A Creative Teaching Guide

Allison Zmuda
and
Mary Tomaino

Foreword by Patricia Wasley

NEA Professional Library
National Education Association
Washington, D.C.

Teachers College
Columbia University
New York and London

Published simultaneously by Teachers College Press, 1234 Amsterdam Avenue, New York, New York 10027 and the NEA Professional Library, 1201 16th Street, N.W., Washington, D.C. 20036.

Library of Congress Cataloging-in-Publication Data

Zmuda, Allison.
  The competent classroom : aligning high school curriculum, standards, and assessment : a creative teaching guide / Allison Zmuda and Mary Tomaino ; foreword by Patricia Wasley.
    p. cm. — (The series on school reform)
  Includes bibliographical references and index.
  ISBN 0-8077-4022-5 (pbk. : alk. paper)
  1. High school teaching—United States. 2. Classroom management—United States.
3. Education, Secondary—Standards—United States. 4. Education, Secondary—United States—Curricula. I. Tomaino, Mary. II. Title. III. Series.
  LB1607.5 .C66 2001
  373.1102'0973—dc21   00-050314

Teachers College Press ISBN 0-8077-4022-5 (paper)
NEA Professional Library ISBN 0-8106-2084-7

Printed on acid-free paper

Manufactured in the United States of America

08 07 06 05 04 03 02 01   8 7 6 5 4 3 2 1

Contents

Foreword

I remember it as if it was yesterday. Thirty-six 16-year-olds and one of me in an American literature class. I had just finished what seemed like a brilliant and extended several-day lecture interspersed with discussion on early American Literature complete with examples from our text and primary sources I'd culled from journals and dusty library stacks. I then described the assignment. Instantly it was clear that the kids did not want to do what I believed to be a deeply engaging piece of work. Slowly, it became apparent that the whole group was not going to do what I wanted them to do. I had two choices. I could insist, conveying that I believed my own professional judgment to be unquestionable, or I could stop and learn from them what the resistance was all about, conveying that they might have legitimate concerns. Either choice seemed frightening.

I remember the feelings I had while comprehending the rebellion. Irritation and anger—because I'd worked so hard to craft something important, something with deep intellectual possibilities, with connections to contemporary life, with threads reaching out to a variety of disciplines and domains; frustration—because I could feel THEIR frustration and I knew that they were generally curious and interested in learning, so that what seemed great to me must, in fact, have a few flaws. It is moments like these that make teaching so incredibly unnerving. At the same time, it is moments like these that make teaching worth doing.

I relived this moment while reading Allison Zmuda and Mary Tomaino's book, *The Competent Classroom*. Good books have a way of illuminating incidents so that one's own experiences come in to sharper focus. This was certainly the case for me while reading this accessible and very important book.

What Allison and Mary do in this book is to reveal what it means to operate as a professional teacher. Working collaboratively, they agree to challenge each other and to hone and refine their skills as teachers. They then proceed to analyze their work with students to locate problems. In this case, they find their grading system to be problematic. After delineating the nature of this particular problem thoroughly, they search for potential courses of action. What follows unfolds just like an authentic teacher's mystery. No single solution is ever adequate for a complex problem. In addition, any change, such as a change in assessment strategies, affects everything else—curriculum, pedagogy, and standards—so that multiple adjustments need to be made. Allison and Mary reveal what they did first, where that led them, what happened next, why that wasn't good enough, and so on until they create a solid, interconnected approach to working with students.

They also show that such refinement takes considerable time. Throughout we hear the voices of students who help their teachers clarify the issues, the complexities and the path toward deeper learning. They worked on this particular course for 3 years before they felt all the pieces of the puzzle had come into alignment.

During my lifetime in schools, educators have marched in a regular, if changing, parade of foci all aimed at improving student learning. In the 1960s it was "more relevant" curriculum; in the seventies, instruction; in the eighties, assessment; and in the nineties, standards. In all that time we believed that if we just tackled that one particular dimension of teaching, problems with learning would be solved. As I have studied teacher's work lives, students' work, and issues related to school change, it has been increasingly apparent to me that we need to attend to all four dimensions at once in order to provide solid, exciting, and enriching experiences for students. This book demonstrates how two teachers pushed themselves to make sure that they provide a substantial and coherent approach for learning about our American past.

Allison and Mary offer a richly interconnected and coherent view of teaching. And somehow they make it seem possible that by holding a steady course, by working to establish the links, we can have schools where kids feel enormously competent.

Patricia Wasley
University of Washington

Acknowledgments

First and foremost, we would like to thank our American Studies students who were the inspiration for all our efforts. We began this journey so that we could do better by you: to create a learning environment where you believed in your own academic success.

Our thinking about teaching and learning has benefited enormously from our conversations with Dr. Robert Kuklis, Assistant Superintendent of Newtown Public Schools. We thank him for having the foresight and patience to enable us to wrestle with these concepts in the classroom and in our writing. His faith in what we wanted to accomplish and his tireless efforts to help us clarify our ideas made this book a reality.

We have been fortunate to be supported along our journey by the teachers, administrators, and staff members of the Newtown Public Schools. Their friendship, professionalism, and constructive criticism strengthened our ability to communicate with teachers across disciplines and grade levels. We especially want to acknowledge Dr. Carmen Jensen for working through our early drafts, Jeanetta Miller for her engaging and thoughtful conversations on teaching and learning, and William Manfredonia for his endless enthusiasm and support for our efforts.

Thank you to Susan Liddicoat and Carole Saltz of Teachers College Press and to Pat Wasley of the University of Washington for taking a chance on two novice authors. Your thoughtful and constructive support kept us moving forward in translating our journey into a broader narrative.

Our heartfelt appreciation to the people who inspired each of us to become teachers in the first place: Gertrude Bucko, Gillian Epstein, Susan Epstein, the late John Huebenthal, Beatrice Jacobson, Jane Lyman, Joseph Macaluso, Edie MacMullen, and Kevin McCarthy.

Finally, to our respective husbands Thomas Zmuda, a phenomenal teacher in his own right, and Richard Tomaino for their love, support, and patience.

Introduction:
Chronicling the Journey

As we looked out upon a sea of 43 new faces, felt the tension in our stomachs and the excitement of unexplored potential in the room, we began the journey all over again. It was the first day of school late in August of 1998: the first day of a new relationship between "us" and "them." Although we had always looked forward to this moment, never had it been so poignant and so dear as it was this time. For the first time in both of our careers, we felt prepared for our students.

Preparation for a teacher is a complex concept. In the beginning of our careers, it meant having our lesson plans in order, complete with a litany of objectives and corresponding activities. Once the lesson plans were in place and the course material felt comfortable, we next focused on making the class an interesting place for students—an environment that fostered learning, self-direction, and original thought. We then struggled to understand why some students just "do not get" the value of our plans and the quality of our ideas. Some years, a few students baffle us with their lack of effort or understanding. Other years, entire classes may fall short of our expectations, both academic and otherwise. Teachers respond to the failure of their students in a variety of ways, from adding innovative activities, to reading current education publications on today's student, to readjusting their own understanding of what to expect from their students. These short-term adjustments reap long-term consequences: a pattern of peaks and valleys, more dependent on the luck of the schedule than the spirit of the learning environment.

BEGINNING THE COURSE

We had begun this roller-coaster ride 3 years earlier. One of us was a graduate of the state university system, entering her thirtieth year of teaching English. The other, who was starting year three, had majored in American Studies at an Ivy League school. What we shared were beliefs and aspirations that helped us mold ourselves into a team, and the philosophy and culture of a district whose adopted motto is "continuous improvement." During the 1996–97 school year, we teamed up to teach American Studies together. This junior elective, designed to meet the goals of the U.S. history and American literature curricula while also providing a rigorous college preparatory experience through the interdisciplinary approach, was only in its fourth year. The course was at a critical point in its development as teachers and administrators scrambled to justify its value to the local community. Teachers in this program faced an array of new challenges, including block scheduling, integrating two curricula, ensuring that all department requirements were met for the eleventh grade, and coordinating teaching styles and personalities.

As we sat together and mapped out the course that first year, we quickly discovered that we had similar perspectives about what the course should look like and how we wanted to teach it. We believed in creating a "truly American Studies experience" by creating a curriculum structure that was greater than the sum of its parts. In other words, we wanted to construct an intellectual framework that was more than a combined English and social studies course. Our course would ask students to examine American culture by looking at historical movements and events as well as significant works of American authors, poets, and artists. We believed that a true testament to our success would be to be able to keep one grade book and to have students forget which teacher represented which department.

Emboldened by our common perspective and our lofty aspirations, we introduced our vision to our class of 32 college preparatory students. As we surveyed them that first year and reflected on the ambitious course we had designed, we wondered whether or not we were asking too much. Our students ranged from having reading skills on the postsecondary level to skills barely on the middle school level; while some of our students reveled in writing assignments, others found difficulty translating their thoughts onto paper. Meeting the range of skills and interests immediately proved to be a concern as we worked to help all students meet the course objectives. Although we had a sense that there were problems with our initial expectations and selection of materials, we brushed aside these "shortcomings" with the understanding that these kinds of problems always happen during the first year of a course. "Things will get better next time, when we have ironed out the rest of the problems, when we really know what this course should look like from beginning to end." We were elated by the intellectual challenges of the course for the students and by the professional benefits of teaching together. We were learning, along with our students, about how this course could push all participants deeper into the study of American history and literature by asking bigger questions and having the time to look to a wider variety of places for answers.

THE COURSE UNRAVELS

By the winter of 1996–97, however, the shortcomings of the current course design began to overshadow the intellectual joys. Our students were working hard but were growing increasingly frustrated with our short-term and long-term expectations. Although both teachers and students liked one another as people, we were finding it difficult to meet one another's needs. We asked our students to work through a difficult piece of reading; they asked us why it was significant. We asked them to compare and contrast different perspectives; they asked us why it was necessary to drag out the process. We asked them to complete a fascinating intellectual task; they asked us why we could not tell them the answer. We were unhappy that they found it necessary to complain about every task we assigned them to complete.

Despite class meetings, long explanations justifying each assignment, and other communication tools, we found ourselves at odds with our students on a regular basis. Our experience with Jane was typical. As we looked over Jane's essay on the consumer culture of the 1920s, we knew that she was not going to be pleased. This was Jane's second attempt at the assignment, and this draft had more problems than the original. When we called Jane over to discuss the issues that still needed to be worked on, she exploded. "I can't believe that I wasted my weekend to do worse! I don't know why I even bother to try in this class. No matter what I do, I can never get higher than a B–. You probably don't even read my work any more." With that, Jane stormed back to her seat to her waiting friends, who then began to commiserate about how unfair we were and how much they hated the class.

After school that day, we sat down together to review what had happened. It was mid-December, and we were rapidly losing the cooperation of our students. They were genuinely frustrated with the course and with us. They believed that we gave them too much work, not enough time to complete the work, and then, to top it all off, graded them in an unfair manner. Although we cared what our students thought, their complaints had grown tiresome and their lack of effort had made us unsympathetic to their comments. Jane was a perfect example. We had taken the time to write out comments to her explaining why she had earned a B– on the first draft and had suggested ways in which she could improve her writing. Instead of taking our advice, she crumpled up the first draft and decided to start over again. As educators we knew that it was our job to help our students continuously improve, but we were beginning to feel as if we were expending more energy on this task than our students. We needed to find a method to increase personal engagement with their own learning (Sizer, 1984).

We were in gridlock and knew that we had to find a way to ease the mutual frustration that congested our classroom. The following day, we sat down with our students and told them for the next 42 minutes we just wanted to listen to their concerns about the class. All we would do was write down what they said. Amidst the general grumbling, a common theme quickly emerged—they were angry with us not because we expected a lot of them, but because they did not understand how to be successful. Frank explained the crux of the matter in his usual blunt fashion: "Do you really expect us to work hard in here if we know that we are not going to do well?" We were taken aback not only by the pessimism of the comment but also by the number of heads that nodded in agreement. When asked why they felt this way, there was a range of student responses:

"Not enough time to complete the assignments!"

"I never understand what the essays have to do with all of the readings and discussions we have during the unit. Why can't you make them relate more to one another?"

"Your directions are OK, but I have no clue why I get the grade I get. The times I think that I did bad, I do good, and the times where I really try, you don't like what I write."

"I understand what I have to do when you explain it in class, but when I am at home staring at my computer, I feel totally lost again."

"How do you really grade our work? Do you just know what we are going to get after the first paragraph, or do you actually take the time to read what we wrote?"

Forty-two minutes and seven pages of notes later, we had a much clearer understanding of the problem. First, we needed to admit to ourselves that despite our efforts to create a rigorous and interesting experience for our students, the course was not working for them or for us. We needed to re-build the goodwill in the classroom, or it was going to be a very long and unproductive school year.

Second, the vast majority of students really did not understand the rea-soning behind their assignments. They understood the issues in class dis-cussions and the points of view described in primary and secondary docu-ments, but they were unsure what to do with all the different pieces. Although the essay questions and project-based assessments were designed to have them put these pieces together to construct an overall thesis statement or position, they felt overwhelmed by the request. Upon reflection, their ap-prehension was not surprising. No matter how rigorous or interesting a task was, we were engaging them in mystery learning. Although we had always distributed culminating assignments at the end of each unit, our students were telling us that they wanted to know exactly what was expected of them sooner. They did not appreciate or appear to benefit from the drama of train-ing for a goal without knowing what the goal was.

Third, our students felt uninvolved in the grading process. They honestly did not understand how we graded their work. Old-time myths ranging from throwing papers down the stairs to just writing down whatever we felt like still danced around their minds as half-truths. They sincerely believed that they were *given* grades by their teachers, not that they *earned* them. In addition to their concerns, our own feeling about the course and our students also was at stake. We had prided ourselves on our efforts to be fair, efficient, and conscientious graders and felt disheartened by our students' comments in this area. We were frustrated with them because of the amount of time and energy we spent evaluating their work and our commitment to helping them improve their work by meeting with them outside of class and accepting revisions of every assignment.

REVISING THE COURSE

It was clear that we needed to develop a new system of evaluating student work that channeled the energy expended by both student and teacher into a more fair, comprehensive, and efficient framework. We believed that the key to student motivation was unveiling the mystery around the game of scoring student work and empowering them with our own train of thought when we evaluated their assignments. After one of us attended a national conference on rubrics that February, we believed that this scoring approach would be the answer to our prayers. We learned that a rubric was simply a scoring system that communicates to students the criteria by which a task would be evaluated. According to the leaders of the conference, if teachers wrote a rubric that articulated what an A paper, a B paper, a C paper, and so forth looked like, then students would be empowered to choose their own achievement levels. Grades would not be a punishment, but a fair and just reward for those who cared enough to invest effort into the class. Our students finally would feel free and competent with us—liberated from the tyranny of the red pen. Even though we expended tremendous effort and energy in creating rubrics, the result was a complex and convoluted system that was difficult to operate and even more difficult to justify.

As we waited for and worked toward a new evaluation system, we were surprisingly side-tracked by another aspect of our classroom—the curricular framework of the course. We volunteered in April of 1997 to attend a conference centered around the work of the Secretary's Commission on Achieving Necessary Skills (SCANS) to learn about how school-to-career objectives could operate in every classroom. Although the workshop was largely attended by Fine and Applied Arts teachers, we immediately saw the relevance and significance of the school-to-career objectives in our own classroom. The presenters at the workshop posed two simple questions that would take us several months to begin to answer. First, what did we want to teach? Second, what do we want our students to learn? They challenged us to decide what was most valuable to us in the courses we taught and to communicate those concepts to students.

We initially thought that it would be impossible to narrow down our 183-day, double-period, double-discipline course to several key concepts, but we began tinkering with the idea on our notepads. The challenge we faced was how to craft a minimal number of questions, called essential questions, that would focus and direct student study without limiting the scope of the course. Although the presenters repeatedly reminded us that we should pace the course based on student understanding rather than curricular schedules, we still struggled to reconcile the amount of information we "needed" to cover with the more time-consuming, but intellectually attractive, concept of establishing curricular values in the classroom. By the end of the afternoon, we had written a few core values reflecting both skill focuses and content areas that we believed represented the heart of the course.

It was more than 3 months before we glanced at our workshop notepads again. We had decided after the workshop that it was too late to restructure the course at that point in the school year and to wait until the summer, when we could devote our full attention to the endeavor. This would prove to be one of the most intelligent choices we made. We strongly believed that the distractions and demands during the school year made it difficult for us to follow through on our ideas. Thanks to the financial and professional support of Bob Kuklis, our assistant superintendent, we received funding for the summer to reshape our entire curriculum to determine what we valued most in American Studies and how to communicate and instill those values in our students.

By July of 1997, we had created essential questions and content standards for the entire course. We literally had sweated out the process, working together for more than 80 hours in the summer heat. The result was gratifying, though, because we felt that we had written questions to direct the study of each marking period that were broad enough to cover all our intended curriculum, and interesting enough to stimulate student involvement throughout an entire quarter. They would provide focus and unity to all the work that we did for 9 weeks at a time. Pleased with our work, we decided to reinforce the importance of these driving questions to our students by including the questions on the instructions sheet for each major assignment. In the middle of this relatively mindless inputting task, we came to an uncomfortable realization: Our essential questions did not exactly fit some of our favorite project-based assessments and writing assignments. To put it more bluntly, the completion of the assignment would not help our students to respond directly to the essential questions for the marking period. We were not prepared for the fact that our 4-day brainstorming session would wipe out most of our work of the past year.

As we sat sulking about our latest predicament, we slowly came to appreciate the implications of our latest brainstorm. Although we had considered our curriculum development work a separate entity from our goal to improve our grading system, the interplay between the two areas would prove to be the answer to our problems. If we established and articulated the connections between the essential questions of the curriculum and the tasks that students were asked to complete, we would be able to tie the grading system to student performance in answering the question. The use of essential questions would boost the confidence of students who were insecure about the quality of the work they produced outside of the classroom. The next step became constructing assessments that asked students to address the essential questions. We were unpleasantly surprised, however, to discover that many of our favorite assignments did not ask students to wrestle with key values and concepts of the course, and abandoned them for the sake of preserving the preeminence of essential questions in the course. We believed that if the project-based assessments required students to construct the link between the broad essential questions and the specific time period covered in the unit, they would have a broader base for comparison with prior work they had completed (since it also was centered around the same question) and would feel less overwhelmed because they were applying a familiar theme to a new topic.

TESTING OUR PLANS

As we began the course again in the fall of 1997, we were cautiously optimistic about testing the viability of our standards-based work. When we first wrote standards during the summer, they seemed to offer a dramatic improvement over the rubrics and assessment checklists that we had relied on throughout the previous year. In addition to working with curricular and evaluation issues, the 1997–98 school year resulted in new challenges, including larger class sizes (one section of 35 students and one section of 41 students) and a temporary classroom in a lecture hall (no other room in the school was available that could seat all of our students). After doing our first-day diagnostic check to determine the skills and prior knowledge of our students, we once again were struck by the tremendous range of academic abilities in the same classroom. We knew that now, more than ever, we needed a clear and effective way to communicate to our students what the course expectations were, why they were important, and how they could meet them.

Much to our delight, our students quickly understood the core values of the course and began working to answer the essential questions and to meet or exceed the standards for each assessment. Standards became the communication tool to express to students what we value not only for each task but also for the course, for the content area, and for the skill focus. We developed a grading system that informed students from the beginning about what we expected from them and how many points we attached to those expectations. We also redefined success in our classroom, abandoning the traditional grading model for a new measuring stick: achieving standard. We wanted students to change how they envisioned their own performance: No longer could students choose to "just get by" in our classroom.

WHY IT WORKED

Although we had thought for months that the performance standards had been successful because the concept revolutionized the grading process, we came to realize in the fall of 1998, our third year of teaching the course together, that the standards worked because they were part of our overall effort to keep curriculum, assessment, and evaluation in alignment. We knew that researchers into school reform were recognizing that pedagogy and assessment were inextricably linked (Wasley, 1994). This epiphany came to us as we marveled at our students' insights into class materials and early understanding of the first marking period's essential question. With an average class size of 43 students, one-quarter of whom were either special education clients or covered by the Americans with Disabilities Act, we expected to struggle to keep all students on target. However, our students continued to feel empowered by truly understanding what their teachers expected from them, why we had those expectations, and how to meet them. Out of 76 students during the 1997–98 school year, not one student failed our course. Once again in 1998–99, 100% of our students passed the course, many of them receiving the highest social studies and English grades of their high school careers.

Over the span of several years we had unwittingly transcended our work to improve the game of scoring in search of a higher sense of competency. We refocused our efforts on creating a reciprocal arrangement between what we value as teachers and what our students value as learners. This shift turned our one-sided pontifications into a mutual relationship in which both the teachers and the learners felt competent in the classroom. Although the development and use of performance standards played a crucial role in communicating what values drive our evaluation of student work, the reason they were so effective was that they reinforced the values of the curriculum. We had found a way to pursue challenging, open-ended intellectual questions without frustrating the goodwill of our students. By keeping the curriculum, assessment, and performance standards in alignment, all classroom participants feel confident that they know why they are here and what they are searching for. We have learned through experience that focusing on only one of these three elements as a panacea will produce limited success in the classroom. In fact, if your experiences as a teacher are similar to ours, even if you try to focus on one aspect, your exploration will bring you to the other two. If you can endure the discomfort of reassessing why you are teaching the course, articulating those values, and ensuring that those values are evaluated by relevant assessments and fair performance standards, the possibilities are endless.

OVERVIEW OF THIS BOOK

This book is designed to help teachers achieve greater success in the classroom through alignment of curriculum to produce focus, purpose, and unity in teaching and learning. Chapter 1 delineates our vision for "the competent classroom" and links this vision to current educational research and development in standards-based education. Chapters 2–6 expand on the concepts that are described in Chapter 1 through conceptual overviews, examples, classroom anecdotes, and self-reflection. Chapters 7 and 8 deal with continuous improvement, ways to expand on and refine the ideas of the competent classroom. We have included throughout the text the responses and feedback we received from our students to show how the concepts explained in Chapter 1 translated into the classroom. Student names have been changed to preserve their anonymity. We hope our own experiences will provide you with the pragmatism and idealism necessary to navigate this course.

Appendix A includes two versions of the American Studies curriculum to demonstrate how we aligned essential questions, content standards, assessments, and performance standards in our classroom. Appendix B contains several instructional tools to help you write and use performance standards.

Although creating alignment in a classroom was not easy, it was by far the most intellectually stimulating and professionally rewarding endeavor of our careers. Because of the extraordinary results we achieved through this reform, we want to share it with other teachers. Through our experience in presenting workshops to educators, we are convinced of its applicability to a broad range of students on both the primary and secondary levels and in all curricular areas, such as math, English, foreign language, science, social studies, physical education, special education, ESL, adult education, and agricultural studies. Our underlying premise is the belief that teachers can make clear to their students "why they are here." Most teachers agree that their students do not understand the core values and essential questions that drive the curriculum of the course. Educators also agree that, if students have a clearer understanding of these core values and essential questions, it would be a major step in improving the quality of critical thought, discussion, and student performance. In addition to refocusing the curriculum to clarify essential questions and content standards, teachers need to take the final steps of supporting the curricular requirements through the creation of performance standards to evaluate student work. In the chapters that follow, we demonstrate how to take these major steps and build a competent classroom.

THE COMPETENT CLASSROOM

CHAPTER 1

What Does a Competent Classroom Look Like?

UNDERSTANDING KEY TERMINOLOGY AND CONCEPTS

The competent classroom is a focused and "thoughtful" place (Sizer, 1986, p. 40). In a competent classroom, teachers and students work in a partnership, united in teaching and learning. Grades are not a punitive exercise of teacher power, but instead a constructive and predictable reflection of how well the student meets the standards for the task, unit, and course. This chapter introduces the components of a competent classroom, each of which is discussed in more detail in subsequent chapters. These four components are:

- Essential questions
- Content standards and instructional objectives
- Assessments
- Performance standards

When all four are in alignment, the learning environment becomes a more dynamic, exciting, and enriching place for both teacher and student: They feel competent in the classroom. Every component of instruction interlocks with every other component, producing a classroom with a consistent sense of purpose and direction.

ESSENTIAL QUESTIONS

The cornerstone for creating this sense of purpose is the essential question because it communicates to classroom participants what we care about (Sizer, 1992). An essential question provides the focus for a unit or course in language accessible to both student and teacher. This simply phrased question is broad enough and interesting enough to stimulate thought in many directions. To develop essential questions, teachers need to reexamine the heart of the curriculum and supplementary activities to determine what they want to teach and what they want students to learn. Some examples of essential questions that we have used to focus and direct our courses are the following:

- What does it mean to be a nation? (U.S. History)
- What does it mean to be human? (World Literature)
- Would you die for your country? (American Studies)
- Are we in it for the money? (American Studies)

We work and rework our essential questions because they focus where our entire course is going. They provide students with an intellectual question that they feel they can already answer but that will stimulate them to go ever deeper into course materials to refine their answers. They will have to answer the essential question with all the resources at their disposal at the end of the course.

Essential questions provide several benefits to classroom instruction. The first is that the initial understanding that students feel they possess increases their sense of power, one of the five basic human needs discussed by William Glasser (1986). Also, all their instruction leads to answering the essential question, so as David Kobrin succinctly put it, "Human beings tend to like manageable challenges" (1992, p. 138). Second, an essential question establishes a perspective for a course or unit. Theodore Sizer ascribes to the aphorism "Less is more" (1986, p. 40), on the theory that most courses try to do too much. There is too much to teach and to learn; other researchers agree that schools and teachers need to set priorities about what is important and make tough choices (Tucker & Codding, 1998). Linda Darling-Hammond concurs: "Frameworks are likely to be most useful when they focus on a relatively small set of truly important core ideas" (1993b, p. 232). The essential question's constant focusing of classroom activity ensures against a curriculum "via textbook publishers" (Tucker & Codding, 1998, p. 76) whose only coherence comes from its table of contents.

CONTENT STANDARDS AND INSTRUCTIONAL OBJECTIVES

The second component of curriculum is the content standard(s). Content standards are fixed goals for learning that lay out what students should know and be able to do—the knowledge and skills essential to a discipline that students should learn. Student performance in the course is measured according to these fixed standards (Mitchell, Willis, & the Chicago Teachers Union Quest Center, 1995). Since demonstrating mastery of content standards is a benchmark of success in the course, it is important to write standards clearly and definitively, because they direct and delimit the learning activities of the course. Once we had focused our inquiry via our essential questions, we wrote content standards to represent what students actually had to learn as the course went on. What would they need to know in order to give a reasoned and comprehensive answer to the essential question? Effectively written content standards should

- Be specific enough to provide a vision of experience relative to a curriculum
- Be aligned with performance standards, assessments, and principles of learning, curriculum, and instruction
- Be clear and understandable to teachers, students, and parents
- Be assessable in a variety of ways (Hansche, 1998).

From the beginning, we felt that content standards should be few in number. As we completed further curricular revisions, we reduced our content standards for each marking period to one, broken down into a few instructional objectives, each of which represented elements of the content standard. Taken together the instructional objectives serve as the tools to ensure that students experience the delineated content or skill areas. These objectives allow the teacher to plan out the classroom journey for the given unit or course by mapping out the process of learning in order to achieve the fixed goal. The interplay between the content standard and instructional objectives can be seen in the most recent revision of our American Studies curriculum, shown in Figure 1.1.

ASSESSMENT

The third piece of our aligned framework is assessment, which we define as providing students with the opportunities to demonstrate their understanding of the essential question and content standards. Assessments include any and all examinations, tests, quizzes, and performance tasks that teachers use to measure how their students are learning. Our original forays into curriculum revision had been in the direction of creating performance standards for our assessments. Like most hardworking teachers, we thought we had a repertoire of challenging, successful, and fun assessments. A deeper look at our existing assessments revealed that many of them were out of alignment with the essential question and the content standards. Doing the assessments would not help students to answer the

Figure 1.1. Example of the Relationship Between Content Standard and Instructional Objectives

Content standard:	The student will be able to determine the degree to which materialism colors individual and collective action.
Instructional objectives:	The student analyzes the impact of the Industrial Revolution on American life.
	The student examines the evolving importance of the consumer in American culture.
	The student evaluates the tension between materialistic ambitions and social conscience.
	The student explores the aesthetic response to dramatic economic changes.
	The student evaluates how forms of expression shape public opinion.

essential question or demonstrate their understanding of the content standard. Research has shown that

> people learn best when they make connections between what they already know and what they are learning, when they can draw on their experiences and make greater meaning of them, when they can see how ideas relate to one another, and when they can use what they are learning in concrete ways. (Darling-Hammond, 1993b, p. 55)

This can happen only when the assessment the student is asked to complete has a direct link to the essential question and the content standard. Also, by the alignment of the essential question, content standard, and assessment, we fulfill one of Glasser's conditions for quality school work: Students should only be asked to do useful work (1992). At the simplest level, an assessment should be useful in helping students to answer the essential question and demonstrate understanding of the content standard, thereby earning success in the course. At a higher level, carefully thought-out assessments should be useful in such ways as developing habits of mind, problem-solving strategies, and higher-level thinking skills.

PERFORMANCE STANDARDS

Creating effective performance standards is the final step in curricular alignment. The process begins with an essential question, which establishes a driving force and perspective for the marking period. Next, the creation of a strong content standard and the breakdown of that standard into instructional objectives define and focus classroom instruction and activities. Third, well-thought-out assessments provide the student with opportunities to demonstrate understanding of the essential question and mastery of the content standard and instructional objectives. Performance standards fit neatly into that framework as a necessary last step.

Performance standards inform the student as to what his or her work should look like. They describe levels of performance and/or evidence that the content standards have been met. It has been said that "the standard is equal to the crossbar in pole vaulting; it is an agreed-upon level of accomplishment that students must reach" (Wasley, Hampel, & Clark, 1997, p. 108). We found that performance standards produced truly dramatic results in our classroom when they, too, were in alignment with essential questions, content standards, and assessments. "Most American adolescents want to learn, and they appreciate sensible standards. They are eminently teachable as long as they are respected" (Sizer, 1992, p. 199).

BUILDING CURRICULAR ALIGNMENT

To demonstrate the effectiveness of curriculum that is in alignment, we include here two examples of assessments. The first is the semester examination used in American Studies in June 1999 as a culmination of the marking period on America's wars (see Figure 1.2). The students' task was to choose the war that had the greatest impact on America's self-image and in an oral presentation discuss that war in terms of both history and literature.

The students had to answer the essential question for the marking period by their justification of their choice of an American war. In addition, they had to demonstrate that they understood the quarter's content standard: The student will be able to assess the impact of war on the United States. The performance standards for the assessment linked directly to the essential question, content standard, and instructional objectives. Although they did not receive the actual assignment, students were told on the first day of the marking period that this would be their final assessment, so they spent the weeks studying America's wars with an eye to answering the essential question with one war. Needless to say, although putting the

FIGURE 1.2. **Final Examination on American Wars**

Essential Question
How does war shape the self-image of America?

Directions
Each student will deliver an 8–10 minute oral presentation addressing the question: *Which American war had the greatest impact on our nation's self-image?* To answer the question, select one of the following wars we have studied this marking period:
- American Revolution
- Civil War
- World War I
- World War II
- Cold War (Korea and Vietnam)

Your oral presentation must include the following components:
☞ Discussion of three of the six essential questions the class developed about war
☞ Discussion of U.S. domestic and foreign policies before, during, and after the war
☞ A poem that you wrote on the war
☞ An analysis of the movie you saw on the war
☞ Two primary source references about the war
☞ Discussion of your independent reading on the war

SUGGESTED TIME	ORAL PRESENTATION COMPONENTS
1 minute	Introduction • Overview on why you selected this war
2 minutes	What made America go to war? • Address essential question • Explanation/quotations from two primary sources • Poem on war
3 minutes	How do artistic/literary expressions of war shape our understanding? • Independent reading about the war • Movie about the war
2 minutes	Conclusion • Domestic impact of the war • Foreign policy impact of the war • Why the war made it the most significant in shaping our nation's image

(*continued*)

Performance Standards

Standard is set at an 82. A check plus = +2; a check minus = −2.
A zero (−10) will be given if the student's work does not address the requirements of the standard.

1. The student includes all of the required sources in his or her discussion of the war. (NOTE: You cannot exceed standard here.)
2. The student addresses the essential question on what makes a nation go to war.
3. The student uses examples from two primary sources to support his or her answers to the essential questions.
4. The student delivers his or her original poem on the war and draws a connection between the war and the essential questions.
5. The student discusses his or her independent reading selection to demonstrate how literary expressions of war shapes our understanding.
6. The student discusses his or her movie selection to demonstrate how artistic expressions of war shapes our understanding.
7. The student addresses the domestic and foreign policy impact of the war on America.
8. The student's discussion of the war he or she selected demonstrates why he or she believes it had the greatest impact on our nation's self-image.
9. The student makes an effort to sustain the interest of the audience through the use of consistent eye contact, volume, speaking pace, and energy level.
10. The student organizes his or her ideas (and provides organizational cues) so that the audience can follow his or her train of thought.

---

oral presentation together presented real challenges, at no point did it engage the students in mystery learning. Two distinct benefits occur when learning is demystified: "Demystification empowers students to succeed while increasing their own responsibility to do so" (Darling-Hammond, Ancess, & Falk, 1995, p. 50). They know in advance what to do and what sources they will need to use to perform well, but they are also pressed to act independently.

The second example, done at the same point in the school year, is the portfolio, a requirement of every English student in the school (see Figure 1.3). It could have been a standard English portfolio, but when we created this assessment, we decided to make it a true American Studies assignment by asking students to discuss their own writing in the context of the essential question and content standard for the marking period. Each piece of poetry assigned during the marking period had focused on a single war's impact on the United States. Discussing the body of the poetry required the students to assess the impact of the various wars on America's self-image as well as to critique the poems themselves.

This portfolio assignment was also introduced to students early in the marking period and explained at length later on. Once again, they knew

FIGURE 1.3. **Retrospective on American Wars: A Portfolio for American Studies**

Essential Question
How has war shaped the image of America?

Overview
During the fourth marking period, we examined the way that war has shaped the image of the United States through several media: individual student poetry, film viewing questions, and independent reading of a war novel. Your assignments have helped you to examine and reflect on the many ways that war has contributed to how Americans see themselves, their nation, their politicians, and war itself. Therefore, to demonstrate your understanding of the essential questions and your own personal growth as a writer, you will compile a portfolio of your fourth quarter work in American Studies.

Assignment
You have completed a poem and viewing questions for each of the following time periods:

- The American Revolution
- Manifest Destiny and the Mexican War
- The Civil War
- World War I
- World War II
- The Cold War and Vietnam

Please follow the format below to compile your portfolio:

1. Collect each poem and viewing question sheet from the marking period. You will need to type any poems that are handwritten, and make a clean printed copy of papers that have already been typed.
2. Arrange the papers in the order that they were completed.
3. Choose one poem that you will revise and rewrite for the portfolio. For this paper, attach also the graded copy or copies with performance standards. This piece of poetry will represent your writing process.
4. Write a one-to-two-page Note from the Author, in which you discuss the development of your skills as a poet. How does each piece show how you learned to capture the spirit and convey the emotion of a historical period? How does each piece demonstrate your skill at incorporating historical themes and information into poetry? How skilled have you become at using effective and precise language? How would you improve the pieces you have written? Refer specifically to the individual poems in your discussion.
5. Write a two-page Speculation in which you answer the essential question for the marking period, How has war shaped the image of America? In this speculation, you will concentrate on how literary and artistic expressions (poems, films, and novels) enhance our understanding. Refer specifically to the poems, to the films, and to your independent reading. Talk about what authors and filmmakers have to say about war and how each war has shaped or changed or affected Americans. Discuss what Americans think about war, why we decide to go to war, and how war affects us individually and collectively.

(*continued*)

Format

Organize the portfolio in this order in a folder, binder, or three-ring notebook.

1. Table of Contents: name of each piece and its title.
2. Note from the Author: your reflection on the poems in this portfolio and how they illustrate your development as a writer of poetry, in capturing and conveying emotion, in incorporating historical themes and information into poetry, and in using language precisely and effectively.
3. Writing assignments and viewing questions for the quarter: arranged in chronological order. Remember to include drafts and performance standards for one piece.
4. Independent reading entry slip: include this as the last piece if you have not already submitted it.
5. Speculation: your speculation about the way that war has shaped the image of America, and how literary and artistic expressions help to enhance our understanding of the effects of war on America and Americans. *Refer specifically to your poems, your viewing questions on the films, and your independent reading to write this speculation.*

Performance Standards

Standard for this assignment is 86. A check plus = +2 and a check minus = −2. A zero (−10) indicates that there is no visible evidence of an attempt to meet the standard.

1. The student's portfolio includes all of the assigned pieces. (NOTE: There will be a deduction of ten points for each missing piece. It is not possible to exceed standard here.)
2. The student's table of contents organizes the portfolio.
3. The student's note from the author discusses his or her development in writing poetry and plans for improvement.
4. The student's note from the author refers specifically to the pieces of poetry in the portfolio.
5. The student's speculation refers specifically to the individual wars (using examples from poetry, viewing, and independent reading).
6. The student's speculation discusses the essential question, including how literary and artistic expressions enhance our understanding.
7. The student demonstrates his or her professionalism by proofreading the portfolio to eliminate mechanical errors and by typing all entries.
8. The student accurately self-assesses his or her own work.

---

well in advance what was required, which freed them from needless anxiety and frustration but also put the responsibility for meeting the standard squarely on their shoulders.

We are convinced that much of the success we have enjoyed as team teachers derives from the creation of an aligned curriculum. We believe that

when teachers use content standards, performance standards and assessments that are aligned in a single comprehensive system, instruction becomes more powerful than in a learning context where only details of curriculum are addressed, assessments are generic, and there are no stated goals or standards against which to measure student progress. (Hansche, 1998, p. 11)

The power of the aligned curriculum creates competence in a classroom, where students and teachers are partners, co-owners of the learning process. We adhere strongly to three essential principles of learning:

- Student effort is a more important determinant of achievement than natural ability.
- Getting all students to achieve at high levels depends on clear expectations that are the same for all students.
- All students need a thinking curriculum that combines deep understanding with application. (Tucker & Codding, 1998, pp. 76–78)

In the competent classroom, students hear the essential question on the first day and see that every assignment helps to hone their understanding of the content standard and enrich their perspective on the essential question. There is no code to break, and the student who tries hard can succeed. Expectations, in the form of performance standards, are given in advance to all students, with the assumption that all students can meet them. Also, the alignment of curriculum allows students to explore an intellectual concept deeply throughout a marking period. The essential question provides the focus, while the assessments provide the opportunities to apply new knowledge in a variety of ways.

Essential questions, content standards, assessments, and performance standards form a whole, but a whole that is more than the sum of its parts. The competent classroom operates on a basis of mutual respect and trust because teachers and students have entered into a contract. Paraphrasing W. Edwards Deming, William Glasser (1986) described the teacher in such a classroom as one

> who would see that she had to provide a consistent explanation of the purpose of the subject she was teaching and share with her students the idea that they should think about what they are learning and try to help her find the most efficient ways for them to learn. (p. 90)

Students, meanwhile, grow as learners because they are treated with respect, a vital requirement according to Theodore Sizer (1984):

> High schools must respect adolescents more and patronize them less. The best respect is high expectations for them, and a level of accountability more adult in its demands than childlike. We should expect them to learn more while being taught less. (p. 34)

For a teacher, sustaining the competent classroom is a labor of love. It requires constant vigilance to create and maintain alignment of the curriculum and to honor the contract with students that makes them partners, not opponents, in the learning game. In the chapters that follow, we expand on our own experiences with curriculum revision, our struggles to make the philosophical concepts come to life in a practical setting, and our efforts to improve continuously. One example illustrates the dynamic nature of curricular alignment. The American Studies curriculum that we refined over 3 years served us well, yet a new curriculum was adopted for the September 1999–2000 school year (see Appendix A). The revised curriculum attempts to balance English and history more equally and provide an approach that will be suitable for both honors and college prep levels of student. There are four new essential questions and four new content standards, but the pieces of the framework continue to be aligned. As the first day of school dawned, each teacher was more prepared than ever yet felt the same brief tremors of stage fright, the same mixture of enthusiasm and anxiety, because "quality control is a never-ending process" (Kearns & Doyle, 1988, p. 83). Our vision never permits us to be static; instead, the struggle for continuous improvement contributes to the excitement of the classroom experience.

The quest to establish competence in the classroom requires a flexible approach and a strong tolerance for trial and error. Although our hope in writing this book is to speed up the reform process for others, we continue to remind teachers that it takes time to reproduce this curricular vision in their own classrooms. The vision comes with a price. It will cost like-minded reformers time, a temporarily diminished confidence level, the need to reassess curricular priorities, and a loss of certain tasks and materials that have become irrelevant. But as massive as the costs may seem, the benefits are truly extraordinary. As one of our students adeptly wrote in her year-end portfolio, "This is the first class I have ever taken where I have been treated by my teachers as a learner, a thinker, and a writer. Their use of standards has given me a road map for success not only here, but in the future." Feedback like that provides the motivation to continue to seek out additional strategies to make the classroom a more rewarding place for everyone.

CHAPTER 2

What Drives a Course?

DEVELOPING ESSENTIAL QUESTIONS

Although the original impetus for reform in our classroom was to create a better method of grading student work, we soon came to realize that our students' discontent had much deeper roots than "Why do I always get a B–?" Our American Studies course had taken its form according to a traditional recipe for teachers. "Set a strong foundation" might be its motto. We envisioned the curriculum as a set of blocks that represented individual units. Piled up, those blocks made an entire course. All the blocks corresponded with our overall vision, and therefore we assumed that we were communicating that vision to our students at the same time. Curriculum structure, however, would turn out to be our chief problem. We were looking at the course from a perspective that would not work. The "building blocks" idea was too linear. It had a beginning, a middle, and an end, but lacked an overall cohesiveness. Our first and most important task became to revisit the existing curriculum and to provide that integrity. We needed a unified vision of what we wanted an American Studies course to do—an intellectual and philosophical core from which we and our students could branch out in several directions. Once we had built a curriculum that we felt had structural integrity, then we could focus on being loyal to that structure in the creation of assessments. The very last step would be the selection of a means to evaluate and grade our students. Starting from evaluation would not work. We needed to ensure that evaluation aligned with our perspective and structure.

INSPIRATION TO EFFECT CHANGE

As described in the Introduction, our epiphany came when we attended a regional school-to-career conference in the spring of 1997. The presenters posed two simple questions from the research of the Coalition of Essential Schools: What do you value and want to teach? What do you want students to learn? (Sizer, 1986).

Once we realized that we had put the proverbial "cart before the horse," the first task became to talk about what we wanted to teach. What did we need to do to create a course structure that cohered, that made sense, and that engaged students? Once we had achieved that, we could begin to develop strategies to assess their work.

During the summer we decided to rewrite our curriculum from start to finish. As we began the task, we thought that we were really happy with the way we had structured the four marking periods. Each one covered a single theme in U.S. History: Immigration and the American Dream, Work and Play, Political Movements and Social Reform, and America's Wars. We had already chosen materials and matched up many assignments we used in past years that were relevant to each theme. We were thrilled with this "matching exercise," because our new structure seemed conducive to many of our favorite materials and tasks. Now, we decided to reflect on each of our four piles to attempt to articulate essential questions that would drive the course. Based on our attendance at the conference and our increasingly frequent meetings with Assistant Superintendent Kuklis, we had gleaned that an essential question focused on one idea or concept that we valued and considered important to teach. In addition, it should incorporate language that would elicit maximum student interest and challenge students to think in several directions. If the questions worked, they would preserve our commitment to the core themes we valued, and at the same time infuse the curriculum with intellectually challenging issues that would engage our students.

We rapidly found out how much work that required. A good essential question had to be clear and extremely focused, but it also had to be thought-provoking enough to stimulate student engagement and drive thought and discussion in many directions. It had to have a perspective, yet be inclusive enough that students would be able to use it not only to organize their thoughts about the day-to-day work of the whole course but also to see how perspective shapes all kinds of study. Based on the advice we received, we adopted the following three guidelines for writing essential questions:

1. Create a broad question that students can use to explore a wide variety of topics and ideas.
2. Make the question thought-provoking so that students have an intellectual incentive to address the question.
3. Use simple language so students quickly can internalize the question.

By creating and instituting these "overarching questions," we expected "to provide teacher and student with a sharper focus and better direction for inquiry" (Wiggins & McTighe, 1998, p. 27).

GETTING STARTED

The next step was figuring out how to get started. We have learned both through personal experience and through collaboration with other educators that the most intimidating part of writing an essential question is flushing out the core values that constitute the heart of a given course. Jerome Bruner suggests that essential questions "pose dilemmas, subvert obvious or canonical 'truths' or force incongruities upon our attention" (quoted in Wiggins & McTighe, 1998, p. 28). To prevent ourselves and others from blankly staring at an empty page, we developed the following list of questions to focus the brainstorming process:

1. What are the fundamental skills and/or content areas for which students are expected to demonstrate their understanding?
2. What makes this course, theme, or unit intellectually stimulating?
3. What do we value about this course, theme, or unit (based on the responses to Questions 1 and 2)?
4. How are we currently communicating these values (the answers to Question 3) to our students?
5. How many students understand the message we are trying to communicate in these ways (the answers to Question 4)?

Wiggins and McTighe (1998) also offer useful tips and guidelines for developing essential questions in their book *Understanding by Design* (pp. 26–37).

Another strategy we used to make the task easier was to start with the most comfortable and/or familiar part of the course. Because the fourth marking period had just ended, we started there. That was the marking period devoted to America's wars, so we were looking for questions that would permit us to include what we valued in terms of content but that would not narrow or limit thought. Our first efforts yielded four essential questions:

1. What factors prompted America to go to war?
2. How did American foreign policy evolve through involvement in war?
3. What was the impact of war on the American psyche?
4. How do literary and artistic expressions of war shape our understanding?

Our four attempts were intended to generate provocative areas for inquiry, while at the same time allowing for the inclusion of a maximum amount of content. We would lose nothing by choosing a few perspectives to study, because the unity of vision would prove the old adage true: "The whole is greater than the sum of its parts." A year later, we would revise even more, and the result would be a single essential question for the fourth marking period:

- How has war shaped the self-image of America?

For the other marking periods, we developed comparable essential questions:

- Who is entitled to the American Dream?
- What do work and play say about the quality of American life?
- What is reform?

Once we created the essential question, we needed to examine every one of our existing materials and tasks, with this one question in mind: Were they now in alignment with the sharper focus of the marking period?

In addition to content-based questions, we also decided to write skill-based essential questions. Our experiences with the serious skill building needed by students on the college preparatory level indicated that it would be effective to focus intensely on one set of skills per marking period. For example, we decided to structure the tasks of the first marking period around group work to ease students into the heavy workload of the course and to foster a more collaborative classroom environment. Thus, our skill question for that marking period read,

- How does working with others enhance the quality of thought?

By making collaboration the main skill development focus of the marking period, we could create more specific performance standards to reflect the different elements of this focus area. The primary benefit of this approach was that students had a much higher level of clarity about all the tasks. They understood that in addition to demonstrating mastery of the content area, they were also responsible for meeting the standards established for collaboration. This consistency in focus was tremendously successful, especially with our college preparatory level students, because it gave them an opportunity to achieve a greater sense of competency and confidence, one skill area at a time.

Our initial revelation about essential questions became the revolution. With the introduction of essential questions, American Studies would be both unified and demystified. Because our values were now represented by essential questions, we could go on to write content standards and performance standards that further increased communication between teachers and students. Teaching, learning, and grading would always be parts of a game, but with a difference. The students became partners in the game. Now that both sides knew the rules, students' confidence levels rose when they realized that they were being given the necessary tools to succeed and that the teachers would not arbitrarily snatch back control by changing the rules. They anticipated success, they felt more in control, and they reflected both in ever-increasing success. The narrative that follows demonstrates how essential questions worked in the classroom.

ESSENTIAL QUESTIONS IN ACTION

The bell rang, cutting our debate short over the treatment of immigrants during the Industrial Revolution. While many students delivered passionate speeches on behalf of the immigrants who endured hazardous living and working conditions, other students persuasively argued that the American Dream came at a price of hard work and sacrifice that every immigrant in the New World had to endure. It was only the fourth week of school, and we were already amazed by how well the class was going. As our students focused on answering the essential question for the first marking period: Who is entitled to the American Dream? Not only were they more energized and involved in class work, but we found ourselves more intellectually stimulated by the experiences.

As the course went on, the quality of thought only deepened. The greatest testament to the benefit of our essential questions work was an unexpected turn taken in the fourth marking period for our unit on American wars. Although we had been using one essential question—"How has war shaped the self-image of America?"—a class discussion about foreign policy issues facing the young American republic took our students' critical thinking to the next level. Students were asked to examine four foreign policy situations from 1797 to 1810, such as the impressment of American sailors, the French Revolution, the XYZ affair, and the affair of Citizen Genet, to determine whether the situations were serious enough to declare war against Great Britain or France. Our students were frustrated by the humiliations inflicted on the early American empire by various powers and demanded to know how our government could just watch and do nothing. We answered this question by asking our students another one: "Can you come up with a list of questions that will help you to answer the marking period's essential question—'How has war shaped the self-image of America?'" Ninety minutes later, our students had brainstormed and agreed on a list of essential questions that would provide them with a litmus test for understanding American foreign policy. For example, one of their first questions was: "Are we prepared to fight?" The response to this question alone eased their earlier frustrations with American inaction—our military was simply not strong enough to muster a successful counteroffensive. Other student-crafted essential questions included:

- Is the war worth the price of American lives?
- Won't going to war cost us our national pride?
- What are the primary costs and benefits of going to war?
- Do the majority of Americans support the war?
- Do our obligations/alliances require us to go to war?

Because our students had just had the opportunity to observe how many of their questions needed to be addressed in order for a nation to go to war, we continued to focus our class discussions on them as we covered the War of 1812 and the Mexican–American War. Every assignment asked them to consider our entry into a war as a reflection of those essential questions. Then we began a new unit on the Civil War, on the first day asking our students, "What was the primary cause of the Civil War?" Six hands immediately shot up in the air. We let each student answer the question.

"Slavery."

"How whites treated the slaves."

"Ditto."

"That the South thought they could get away with having slaves."

"Slaves."

"Too cheap to actually hire workers like everybody else did."

Over the next 2 weeks, we exposed our students to primary and secondary source documents that encapsulated a variety of perspectives on life in antebellum America. Students were required to link the key ideas learned from each document to the essential questions they had developed on what makes a nation go to war. Soon, their discussion broadened to also include the lack of industrialization in the southern economy and the cultural differences between plantation and city life. They were learning to be more at ease with the ideas that historical questions did not have absolute answers and that their answers would change based on the perspective they chose to adopt.

If students could come to the realization that the study of history and literature is always shaped by perspective, then our overhaul had done its job. Essential questions worked! Our students were trained to use the question for each unit of study as a cornerstone for their discussions, comprehension of reading assignments, and work on performance assessments. This practice gave many of our students the confidence they needed to follow their train of thought without fear of falling on their faces completely. They found great comfort in studying a historical period or a novel in order to answer a specific question rather than conducting a general examination and being asked a surprise question at the end. Our students knew that when they read a difficult primary source document, somewhere embedded in the language was an answer to the unit's essential question. The focus also proved to be an effective reading strategy, especially for those students with weaker reading comprehension skills. The groundless fear that essential questions would limit discussion and analysis gave way to the realization that an essential question could provide the initial perspective from which students could jump to other perspectives. We continually reinforced the notion to our students that if we asked a different question, their interpretation of a piece of literature or analysis of a political movement would be entirely different. For the first time, our course had a "big picture." The four essential questions for the course had been internalized by the students, who could recite them by heart.

TROUBLESHOOTING CONCERNS ABOUT ESSENTIAL QUESTIONS

Despite the positive responses of our students, we were surprised to find that other teachers at the high school were less receptive to the use of essential questions. One afternoon we were sitting with several of our colleagues during lunch and began to talk about our positive experiences.

One faculty member jumped in, "You mean your students only have to focus on one main idea throughout the entire course? No wonder they like your class. It makes it much easier!"

Another remarked, "Don't they get bored with the question after the first 2 weeks?"

A third teacher quipped, "Where is the intellectual challenge in only one question? Aren't you doing them a disservice when they go to college and they are faced with a barrage of questions?"

We knew that essential questions were working, but these criticisms forced us once again to try to articulate why they were successful. While limiting the essential questions to one main idea did make our class easier for our students, it did not diminish the intellectual rigor of our classroom. The course was easier because the framework provides a sense of daily unity that everything that they were learning was relevant to a key concept. Wiggins and McTighe (1998) support this consistent usage of essential questions: "Essential questions can and should be asked over and over" (p. 28). We had eliminated "mystery learning" from our classroom.

As to the comment about whether or not our students got bored with the essential questions, we responded that it took patience, time, and practice with an intellectual question to really understand not only what was being asked but also how to craft a meaningful and appropriate response.

By keeping the essential question consistent throughout a marking period, we were able to move more quickly through the individual components of the course because students could more readily focus on what "the point" was in each unit.

The final comment about whether or not we had done our students a disservice by limiting their studies to one question for a 10-week period was a serious concern that we had agonized over for several months. Although at first glance it might appear that this approach unnecessarily limited students' intellectual growth, we knew from our experiences in the classroom both with and without essential questions that students were much more focused, interested, and inspired by the questions because they believed in the importance of their work. As Sizer (1992) deduced in *Horace's School*, "School, simply, is about the habit of thoughtfulness" (p. 69). Our students were receiving daily opportunities to practice this habit as they connected short-term tasks to profound inquiry. They came to appreciate that any homework assignment they missed or primary source document they skimmed would diminish the quality of their answer to the question. "Provoke a student into the habit of doing important homework, and his task of becoming a self-propelled learner will be easy" (Sizer, 1992, p. 89).

However, we were still left with the question of whether essential questions were more viable for certain students. We knew our college preparatory students thrived on the structure and focus essential questions brought to the course. They needed to have a jumping off point or a lens through which to examine the plethora of materials. Would a more advanced-level student need the same kind of structure? Would it limit students who perhaps were more self-directed than our own? Continuing our exploration through action-based research, we both developed new curricula in the courses we taught separately. One of us taught Honors American Government, a required senior course. Because this was the highest academic level offered, many of the top graduating seniors were in the class. Essential questions proved to be so successful here that Assistant Superintendent Kuklis encouraged several social studies teachers who also taught the course to work in conjunction with us to write a new curriculum. This curriculum would go on to become a model he used to guide curriculum development throughout the school district.

REFINING ESSENTIAL QUESTIONS

Since we first introduced essential questions in American Studies, we have spent hundreds of hours contemplating the language, sentence structure, and focus of each question. Could we make the concept more thought-provoking? Did the question interest our students on a personal level? Intellectual level? Not at all? The most recent revision of the essential questions was designed to achieve two goals:

- To make the questions more contemporary/relevant to our students' lives
- To make the questions more interdisciplinary

We worked in conjunction with two other American Studies teachers in our school to refine these questions. Even though we had written dozens of essential questions before, for both this and other courses, we went through the same agonizing brainstorming process. First, one of us would think aloud, talking through a proposed idea for a question. We then would toss around different variations of the same idea, working to refine and simplify the language. Although we would hem and haw as we processed the different ideas, when someone uttered the "right" question, it was like magic. The right question captured the essence of the inquiry we wanted students to pursue. This type of question prompted an instant response from the student but also could withstand rigorous analytical use without growing stale. Students also could develop a more informed answer to the question through the use of literature and history. After several days of deliberations, we were astounded by the progress we had made, as shown in Figure 2.1.

Our work has shown us that essential questions not only drive students into the course; they also drive the teachers into it as well. As we clarify the line of inquiry, we also refine the structure of the course. This clarification process has made teaching this course a dynamic, evolving experience as we facilitate our students' pursuit of profound issues through the lens of American history and literature.

FIGURE **2.1. First Revision and Second Revision of American Studies Essential Questions**

Original Essential Questions	Revised Essential Questions
☞ Who is entitled to the American Dream?	☞ What does it mean to be an American?
☞ What is reform?	☞ Who are "we the people"?
☞ How has war shaped the image of America?	☞ Would you die for your country?
☞ What do work and play say about the quality of American life?	☞ Are we in it for the money?

APPLYING ESSENTIAL QUESTIONS
ACROSS LEVELS AND DISCIPLINES

As we gained more experience with the function and format of essential questions in a curriculum, we began to devote more time to that aspect of curricular development in the workshops we conducted for other educators. We originally had been hesitant to discuss essential questions because implementing this type of curricular reform is an extensive and time-consuming endeavor, and we were concerned that the magnitude of revision necessary would dishearten our participants. Yet our discussion of essential questions with these educators has proven to be a rewarding and powerful exchange for both them and us.

Although it usually takes several minutes for the participants to adjust to the idea that a course or unit can be "reduced" to one line of inquiry, they soon begin to draft essential questions for themselves as well as to offer suggested revisions for others' essential questions. Usually, we devote about 10 minutes as a full group to discuss a participant's essential question. The point of this group activity is to generate many questions that work to reflect the main idea the participant is working to capture in a given unit or course.

At a recent workshop, a high school health teacher wanted help designing an essential question that would cover the scope of her curriculum. She focused on the idea of health and started with the question "Why is it important to be healthy?" Her initial question inspired other suggestions by participants:

- Who determines health?
- What does it mean to be healthy?
- Is the body wiser than its inhabitant?
- Is living a healthy life desirable?
- Does a person have the right to be unhealthy?

Different people were drawn to different questions, and this health teacher soon became uncomfortable with the lack of consensus.

"So which one am I supposed to use?" she asked worriedly.

"The one that best meets your needs," we replied. A good essential question complements not only the content focus but also the teacher's style and personality. A teacher who is inspired by more philosophical discussions may choose "Is living a healthy life desirable?" A teacher who is inspired by public policy and government issues may choose "Does a person have the right to be unhealthy?" or "Who determines health?" A teacher whose style is more concrete and sequential may opt for the question "What does it mean to be healthy?"

When the "right" essential question is crafted, it sparks instant energy and excitement in the mind of the teacher. One of the most electrifying illustrations occurred during a presentation we gave at a local university for teachers working on curriculum development. An elementary school teacher was trying to design an interdisciplinary unit on maps and was struggling to come up with one question to tie her ideas together. Her initial idea for an essential question was "Why are maps important?" Once again, we asked the audience to consider the importance of creating a question that was "interesting enough" to stimulate a meaningful discussion from the first day to the last day of the unit or course. Ten minutes and 12 questions later, the group expressed unanimous approval for the question "What does it mean to be lost?" The elementary school teacher was thrilled—she immediately began to outline the interdisciplinary connections.

> I can start with a language arts component where the students can do a creative writing activity answering the question. Then, the students can share their writing with one another and we can generate a list of all of the ways being lost makes us feel (anxious, upset, scared, lonely). That will lead us to a discussion of other people who must have felt those same emotions, like the explorers who came to the New World. The social studies component will be studying those explorers and understanding how their mapmaking helped other people not to feel lost. Finally, the science, math, and art components can be the production of an actual map (to scale) of our school. That way my class can help other students not to feel lost.

As we celebrated the idea together, the elementary school teacher abruptly stopped talking and began to write. While she had tuned out the rest of the presentation, she came up to us at the end and excitedly showed us over three pages of notes. "I love this! I never thought I was going to be able to pull this together. How did you do it?"

Our answer to her was based on our own experience: An effective essential question inspires thought. It inspires teachers to frame the content in a manner that is accessible, engaging, and interesting for their students. It inspires students not only to think within the confines of the given unit's or course's content focus, but also to think as a lifelong learner. An essential question celebrates previously acquired knowledge, provokes participants to want to share that knowledge, and engages them in a line of inquiry in pursuit of a more detailed and broader understanding. We continue to be amazed by the number of parents who come up to us on "Back to School Night" to tell us how "exciting" the course overview sounds and how they "wish" they could take American Studies with their child. While no parent to date has taken us up on our open invitation to come to class, they do often stay to discuss their opinions about a particular question. Purposeful and rigorous inquiry truly electrifies our classroom for all participants.

CHAPTER 3

Are Specific Curricular Goals Aligned with Essential Questions?

DEVELOPING CONTENT STANDARDS AND INSTRUCTIONAL OBJECTIVES

The next step in reconfiguring our curriculum was to compose content standards that encompassed both our "new-fangled," thought-provoking essential questions and our traditional course objectives. In the original American Studies curriculum for our school, written in the early 1990s, the writers had included a litany of objectives for each unit that reflected the different approaches and priorities of as many people as possible. Although this menu approach to unit objectives appeased all the teachers of the course (each teacher simply selected those objectives that were most appropriate to his or her personality and vision), students' learning experiences became as diverse as the teachers themselves. For example, one American Studies teacher devoted several months to a local political action project, while another never even introduced the subject of political action to the class. While flexibility is essential in any curriculum, this level of individual free-dom weakened the overall cohesiveness of the course. Parents also com-plained about the disparity in student experiences:

"Why does my child have to do this substantial project when students on the same academic level with a different teacher aren't required to do so?"

"If you really believed that this activity was so significant, then why don't all teachers do it? Shouldn't this be an established part of the curriculum?"

UNDERSTANDING CONTENT STANDARDS

While we wanted to preserve some level of flexibility in the content standards for the course, we also wanted to establish a more consistent course experience for all American Studies students. In addition to trying to bal-ance these two goals, we also needed to construct standards that were con-sistent with established definitions of a content standard. The most useful definition we found comes from *Learning in Overdrive*: "Content standards are fixed goals for learning. They lay out what students should know and be able to do—the knowledge and skills essential to a discipline that students are expected to learn" (Mitchell et al., 1995, p. 19).

Despite the clarity of the authors, we struggled to grasp what this definition meant and how to apply it. At first, we reasoned that content standards simply were essential questions rewritten to end with a period. We thought that this curriculum-writing thing was a snap and quickly moved on to the next step of the curriculum process. As foolish as this initial approach might sound, it took us several months to realize that we were making a fundamental error. Through discussions with Assistant Superintendent Kuklis and personal reflection, we began to clarify for ourselves the fundamental difference between a content standard and an essential question. While an essential question drove students into the material through a broad-based inquiry, a content standard defined the limits of that inquiry based on the subject materials, skill focuses, and grade level of the course. The following example from the marking period in which we focused on America's involvement in armed conflicts demonstrates the alignment between the essential question and content standard:

> *Essential Question:* Would you die for your country?
> *Content Standard:* The student will be able to evaluate how our response to foreign threats impacts individual lives and American culture.

Not only is the essential question thought-provoking, but all students have a strong opinion about the topic even before the marking period begins. This personal investment drives students into the material to challenge or substantiate their beliefs. The content standard both supports the line of inquiry and defines its scope. The standard clarifies that students will need to analyze this question through the examination of the interplay among foreign threats, individual lives, and American culture.

INCORPORATING INSTRUCTIONAL OBJECTIVES

In addition to being in alignment with the broad scope of the essential question, the content standard also has to reflect the explicit concepts and skills of the instructional objectives. While we had struggled to understand the difference between essential questions and content standards, processing the difference between content standards and instructional objectives came much more easily. The authors of *Learning in Overdrive* suggest that a content standard is a "big idea"; objectives are the components of that idea (Mitchell et al., 1995). In addition to being a smaller part of a larger idea, instructional objectives lay out a sequence for the given unit. Instructional objectives map the process for sequencing lessons and the parameters for incorporating what Patricia Wasley (1994) has referred to as a teacher's repertoire. By steadfastly safeguarding the alignment of instructional objectives and instructional activities, we could ensure a high level of intellectual rigor without sacrificing the range of teaching tools and strategies.

Although the use of content standards was a relatively new concept in our district, virtually all curriculum guides included instructional objectives. However, these guides generally contained two serious alignment problems. First, many curricular guides confused big ideas with smaller ones. "Learning to identify what standards look like in academic subjects is critical to successful standards-driven instruction. . . . Objectives are not standards" (Mitchell et al., 1995, p. 23). Second, almost all curricular guides obscured the relationship between instructional objectives and activities. The typical unit would list a plethora of objectives and then an equally lengthy list of suggested activities. This menu approach blurred the sequence of students' learning experience. Each teacher was expected to mix-and-match objectives and activities to produce a meaningful learning experience for students. The lack of alignment between these two components resulted in activities becoming "games of the day" rather than meaningful learning experiences because students often did not see the relevance of the activity to the overall learning process.

To preserve as much of the integrity of the original curriculum as possible, we decided to work through the original lists of objectives to determine proper placement in our revised structure. We then applied a litmus test to assess the appropriateness of each objective:

1. Is this an objective or a content standard?
2. Is this objective in alignment with the content standard?
3. Is it feasible to include the objective here?

The first question addressed the conceptual differences described in the paragraph above: Each objective should be a smaller component of a bigger idea. The second question required a substantive link between the objective and the content standard. If the objective was not reflected in our content standard, we either broadened the standard, moved the objective to another part of the curriculum, or eliminated the objective altogether. The third question required general reflection on the marking period to determine if we had "bit off more than our kids [could] chew" (Mitchell et al., 1995, p. 24). One of the most painful, but necessary, aspects of this sorting process is that certain objectives almost always must be dropped in order to address the remaining objectives in a meaningful way. Figure 3.1 shows the role of instructional objectives in the curriculum structure from the earlier example of the marking period on American wars.

FIGURE **3.1. Excerpt from Second Revision of American Studies Curriculum**

Essential question:	Would you die for your country?
Content standard:	The student will be able to evaluate how our response to foreign threats impacts individual lives and American culture.
Instructional objectives:	The student examines what factors/principles prompt America to use force.
	The student evaluates how American society responds to perceived threats.
	The student analyzes how patriotism determines form and content of public expression during times of crisis.
	The student explores how dissenting forms of expression attempt to challenge public opinion.
	The student assesses the lessons the public has learned through both our evolving understanding of the crisis and how that crisis is portrayed.

One key difference between our application of essential questions and of content standards and objectives was the level of communication with our students. As described in Chapter 2, we actively used essential questions as a daily teaching tool to involve students in course materials and to hone critical thinking skills. We were not as vocal, however, about the role of content standards and objectives in the classroom. Personally, we believed that these two curricular components provided a focus for our teaching practices and instructional tools. It was our job to ensure that we included activities, discussions, and materials that would give students the opportunity to learn required content and practice required skill areas. The performance standards that we created for each assessment would be the link that communicated to students what it was important to learn from the course. They would directly mirror the corresponding content standards and instructional objectives. If we did our job well and gave students a broad sense of the scope of the unit, as well as clear and specific performance standards, they would not need to be bothered by curricular labels. While this approach has worked well for us, we also believe that it is a personal preference rather than a pedagogical necessity.

Although the concepts of content standards and instructional objectives have been around for years, what was relatively new here was their use in the curricular structure. The content standard focuses the key components of the individual unit into a cohesive curricular goal. The instructional objectives then support that standard by breaking down the smaller skill and content focuses the teacher will address to help students achieve that goal. We continue to have to remind ourselves about the differences between a content standard and an objective and the differences between a content standard and assessment. The only sure-fire trick we discovered was the need to continuously analyze our own work to ensure that we maintained the integrity and focus of each concept.

RECONSIDERING THE PROCESS OF CURRICULAR REVISION

Content standards and instructional objectives can serve as important points of entry for teachers and administrators working to revise current curricula. Through our professional development workshops, we have come to appreciate that essential questions can be an intimidating place to start. One of our colleagues shared her frustration with her revision process: "I spent 4 hours trying to come up with a good essential question, but everything I come up with is either too boring or too off-topic. This whole process doesn't seem to be working for me."

Although our first instinct was to help write a question for her, we now realize that it can be more effective to start with the "nuts and bolts" of the curriculum. The process of going through the existing curriculum to determine whether it is feasible to achieve all the content standards and/or instructional objectives in a timely fashion is a powerful place to start (especially when a team of people are collaborating on the revision process). Once those standards and objectives have been pared down to ensure that the curriculum can be followed in the allotted amount of time and that it will enable students to achieve the necessary content and skill development, it then becomes much easier to try to develop essential questions and assessments.

Using content standards and instructional objectives as a point of entry into the revision process has proven to be most helpful to mathematics and foreign-language teachers. During our workshops, we have found these teachers to be frustrated by their curricular demands because they "just have to cover a certain amount of material or the students won't be able to handle the next level." The significant pressure to cover content first and inquiry second frustrates many teachers in these subject areas. Essential questions may not be the driving focus of the teacher for a variety of reasons. One, certain classrooms are content-driven because of directives from administrators, curriculum coordinators, "high-stakes testing," and/or parents. These directives play a powerful role in the revision process and can make essential questions appear to be too much of a time-consuming indulgence. Second, teachers may not find an essential question that really "works" for them or for their course. While some essential questions are instant hits, others are simply mediocre and do not seem to inspire or to electrify. Third, an essential question may be used as a lens for periodic reflection rather than as a consistent frame of reference. For example, if an essential question for a math class is "How do numbers create order?", the teacher can refer back to this question as a strategy to introduce the concept of nonrational numbers or as a way to reflect on the significance of quadratic equations.

From our own classroom experience and our work with other teachers, we have learned that each individual must achieve a comfortable balance between content and essential questions to empower all classroom participants. However, content cannot drown out educational reform. A French teacher recently said to us that she "couldn't afford to take the time to discuss essential questions with her students" because she "had too many chapters to cover in the textbook." When we asked what would happen if the students did not cover all the chapters, she replied that "they would not be able to handle French III." When we asked her if she could afford to have her students lose their love of the language because they did not have the time to explore the material, she replied, "Unfortunately, I am not paid to get them to love French, I am paid to teach them French."

While this stark comment may speak to the reality in many school districts, we believe that every teacher can work to achieve a more harmonious balance between content and inquiry.

CHAPTER 4

Have Students Been Given the Opportunity to Succeed?

REVISITING ASSESSMENTS

Once we had clarified the content standard and instructional objectives for a unit, the next task was to design an assessment that provided students with the opportunity to demonstrate their intellectual and skill development. Assessment design has been a popular focus for years in educational literature and research. Teachers were encouraged to throw away the scoring machines and bubble sheets and instead incorporate more meaningful evaluation strategies. A "meaningful" assessment asked students to demonstrate their understanding of the unit through hands-on application, writing addressed to an audience, and real-world simulations. In our high school, students built an edible model of *Lord of the Flies*, wrote children's stories on "The Bill of Rights," participated in a scavenger hunt to reinforce Latin vocabulary, and tested the law of gravity on staircases throughout the building. The challenge we faced in our use of performance-based assessments was to distinguish between a wonderful evaluation tool inspired by the curricular unit from a wonderful evaluation tool in alignment with the curricular unit. Once teachers achieve clarity about what they expect students to know and be able to do, students in turn can be more successful in meeting those goals and expectations. As Sizer (1992) observed through the fictitious teacher Horace:

> A mindful school is clear about what it expects of a student and about how he can exhibit these qualities, just as a mindful student is one who knows where he is going, is disposed to get there, and is gathering the resources, the knowledge, and the skills to make the journey. (p. 27)

Through the following classroom anecdotes, it will become clearer how the subtlety of this difference can sabotage the "competent classroom."

ASSIGNING "FUN" PROJECTS

Although Jane had been struggling to express her thoughts in writing throughout the 1996–97 school year, we both remember what she looked like the day she turned in her project on American life in the 1950s. The assignment was to illustrate the postwar American Dream in images and words. Jane had painstakingly designed four advertisements depicting a range of dreams from owning a house in Levittown to defending American soil from the evils of communism. Normally a talkative student during class work, Jane bent her head over the old *Life* magazines as she searched for the perfect pictures to illustrate her ideas. When she came up to us the next morning, her eyes were lit up as she handed over her work. "This assignment was so much fun! I just know that I did well."

Jane's upbeat mood was a pleasant surprise. She was usually less than satisfied when she handed in her work and often frustrated in trying to discern the connection between the assessment and the work we had done in class leading up to the assessment. We wanted to know more about why she felt successful this time so that we could do our best to reproduce the experience. "We are so pleased! What about this project did you like so much?"

Jane replied, "It was cool. For once I understood what you wanted and I was excited to do the work. I can't wait to get my grade back. You are going to be proud of me this time, I'm sure. Why can't all of our work be like this?"

"Well, sometimes it is appropriate for an assessment to incorporate more visual skills, and other times it is more relevant to work on demonstrating understanding through written work," we replied. As Jane bristled at our response, we looked at each other a little dejectedly. It was so nice to see Jane happy about herself and her work. It was important to us to maintain a rigorous skill-building program but also vital to provide opportunities for all students to demonstrate that they had learned the material in more nontraditional formats. During our preparation time later that afternoon, we began brainstorming new project ideas that would make students like Jane feel more successful. We devoted several weeks to developing these new assessments and were pleased with the results.

The next month we introduced the first of these imaginative tasks. Based on our discussions about foreign policy and domestic reactions to Vietnam, we asked students to write a song about the Vietnam war. To get them excited about the task, we played several songs that were popular during the time, such as Joan Baez's "Where Have All the Flowers Gone?" and Country Joe and the Fish's "Fixin'-to-Die Rag." We were sure that students would have a positive response to the assignment because it was "fun"—in other words, they did not have to write a lot and the writing that they did have to do was structured in a medium that they themselves enjoyed. We were shocked at the grousing in the room as they began their work. Bob muttered to Sarah as he left the room that day, "Can you believe this one? Same thing, different day. Except this time we have to set our work to music." Jane looked equally depressed the next morning when she gave us her song.

"Here you go. Keep it as long as you want. I'm sure I missed the boat this time."

Once again, we were surprised by her reaction. "We thought this kind of project was right up your alley. Why do you seem so frustrated?"

Jane shrugged her shoulders. "I didn't understand whether I should write about what we talked about in class, you know, about the gross parts of the fighting and the reasons why we were there in the first place . . . or if we should sing about dead flowers. Whatever. It's over with at least." And with that she went back to her seat.

It took us 2 years to really understand Jane's reactions in both of these situations. All teachers want their students to feel confident when completing their work. They generally believe, however, that for an assignment to be perceived as "fun" by students, it must have a "gimmick" or require less work than usual. We also had subscribed to this belief and had incorporated some really "neat" projects into the course to inspire students when they demonstrated their understanding of key concepts and materials.

BRINGING ASSESSMENTS INTO ALIGNMENT

Many of these clever assessments were dropped when we revised our curriculum to focus on essential questions. We found that the tasks did not provide students with an adequate opportunity to demonstrate their understanding of the essential questions. Although we were very disappointed that they did not quite fit with the questions, we were determined to preserve the focus of the course, even at the expense of projects that prompted some of our students' best (and most enthusiastic) work.

We decided that we would give the essential questions a real shot first, and then play with creating more innovative assessments later. It was critical that we reverse our initial curriculum-building process of first collecting as many resources, materials, and activities as possible, and then determining the core values of the course. Although we had originally understood "backwards planning" to be the project-based assessments we wanted students to be able to complete at the end of the marking period, the concept was more basic. It was a process that involved answering three questions:

1. What kind of graduates do we want?
2. How do we get there?
3. How do we know when we have arrived? (Darling-Hammond, 1993a)

We shifted our definition to make the end result the intellectual product. We expected that our students would be able to craft a quality response to the essential question based on the understanding of class materials, participation in class discussion, and practice through the completion of more minor project-based assessments.

As we analyzed the validity of our assessments, we used the following guideline, which was relatively straightforward but immensely helpful:

- Does the assessment provide the students with the opportunity to address the essential question(s) and fulfill the scope of the content standard?

This question posed no limits to the types of assessments that effectively enable students to answer the essential question(s). The only limitation is that the assessment must be in alignment with the essential question and the content standard. To illustrate this point, we have included a list of assessments we used in our classroom:

Oral	Written	Visual
Speeches	Journals	Posters
Skits	Poetry	Pamphlets
Debates	Short stories	Web page
	Analytical essays	Political cartoons
	Diary or letters	Finding and interpreting
	Persuasive essays	photographs
	Journalistic writing	Advertisements
	Research paper	Graphic organizer
	Resume	PowerPoint presentation
	Responses to questions	
	E-mail correspondence	

We selected the format of the assessment based on the overarching bridge provided by the content standard and the learning process delineated by the instructional objectives for the unit. For example, if we were focusing on the experiences of immigrants during the Industrial Revolution, we chose the more personalized format of a diary so students could meet the factual and affective objectives for the unit. Students used the diary entries not only to outline what it was like to work in the factory (machines, working conditions, health conditions, treatment of labor) but also to search for solace, reinforce individual reasons for coming to America, and find the resolve to return to the factory the next day. Thus, the assessment provided students with the opportunity to replicate classroom experiences in a more in-depth fashion.

We still continue to reexamine our assessments each year to determine whether another approach would better enable students to address the key curricular components. The result of this ongoing reflection has been that many assessments were replaced not because they were inappropriate or vague but because we created an even better opportunity that was more relevant and more meaningful to our students and our curriculum. While this constant change can be disheartening at times, the improvement in our students' quality of thought and understanding of the curricular values continues to motivate our vigilant efforts. By designing assessments to ensure that students will complete "purposeful work," we can maintain high levels of interest and rigor in our classroom (Wiggins & McTighe, 1998, p. 117).

STUDENT RESPONSES TO THE NEW FRAMEWORK

After we introduced essential questions into our classroom, however, we were surprised to see the positive response of students when asked to complete a more traditional assignment. The first marking period of the course focused on the essential question, "Who is entitled to the American Dream?" We first worked with students to define the American Dream and then compared and contrasted the immigrants' vision of "the promised land" with their economic, political, and social opportunities. Before examining the immigrant experience, we looked at the American Dream through Thornton Wilder's *Our Town*. Students were asked to demonstrate their understanding of the play and of the essential question by completing a timed-writing piece articulating and assessing the moral message expounded by Wilder through the life and death of Emily Gibbs.

While the previous year Jane and many of her peers had looked pained when trying to complete the task, this year our students quickly settled into the assignment at hand. For almost an hour, our students had their heads bent over their desks, reflecting on their notes, pulling quotations from the play, and writing their ideas into their blue books. One by one, students began to turn in their five-paragraph essays, relieved to be finished but pleased with themselves.

"How do you think it went?" we asked Bill as he handed in his blue book.
"Piece of cake."
"Carol, how about you?"
"Just what I expected. Although I was surprised that I had so much to say."

When we read over the essays, we were impressed by the quality of the students' analysis of the play and attention to the underlying concepts of myth, reality, and the American Dream. Granted, the students had a long way to go in the organization and mechanics of their writing, but their ideas seemed much more thoughtful than those from the year before. As our students continued to handle the traditional and nontraditional assignments with confidence and produce quality work, we became more and more convinced that assessments were popular with students not when they were easy or flashy or "fun," but when they made sense. If students understood why they were doing what they were doing, they were more likely to invest their hearts, minds, and energies in the task.

PROVIDING A FOCUSED LEARNING EXPERIENCE

By creating an essential question for each marking period of the course, our students became much more aware about the intellectual goal, and we fulfilled another goal of the Quality School—that "a teacher should never surprise [the] students" (Glasser, 1992, p. 19). Our students were told on the first day of the marking period that the final assessment at the end of each marking period would be to answer the essential question. They were also told that every task they completed until the end of the marking period would better inform their answer to the essential question. Therefore, in order to maintain the integrity of this curriculum structure, we had to ensure that every assessment had a clear correlation to the question at hand. This was the only trick necessary in order for students to find meaning in their work. Although we still worked to incorporate a variety of tasks and formats to keep students' interest level high, we did not feel as if the students' needs to do "fun" work conflicted with our needs to create challenging, purposeful assessments.

Not only was keeping the assessments in alignment with the essential questions crucial, but so, too, was the timing of assigning them. Although we had always believed in giving students as much advance notice as possible, we tended to wait until we had almost reached the end of a unit to inform the students about their culminating assessment. Our reasoning had been that they would feel overwhelmed by the task unless they already had a grasp of the core concepts of the unit and had been exposed to most of the materials. Once we began to use essential questions, however, it seemed logical that students should be given the assessment directions when the unit was introduced. If the students already knew what question they were working to answer, the assessment simply became the organizational tool for articulating their response. The threat, not the challenge, was gone from our classroom. Assessments were no longer a dark mystery looming at the end of a tunnel; they were linked to the class discussions and materials on a daily basis until they became familiar and comfortable. Because the assessments were the end of the process mapped out by the instructional objectives, we as teachers had a much clearer understanding about how to sustain the focus and rigor of the learning experience. Once we introduced an assessment to the class, we were constantly reminded to provide students with opportunities to practice both the skills and subject matter every step along the way. While we had always been comfortable including a variety of learning activities and strategies, we were astounded by how much better we were at taking advantage of "teachable moments" and providing students different points of entry into understanding. Our own thinking about the beginning, middle, and end of our lesson sequences ensured a consistent, rigorous, and focused learning experience for our students on a daily basis, not just when an assessment loomed on the horizon.

EXAMPLES OF VALID ASSESSMENTS

To illustrate what assessments now look like in our classroom, we will return to the essential question from the first marking period, "Who is entitled to the American Dream?" After the short unit on Thornton Wilder's *Our Town*, we begin to trace the core waves of immigration to the United States. For organizational purposes, we created four units of study:

2000 b.c.–1820: Early Immigrants (Native Americans, Europeans, and Africans)
1820–1880: Old Immigrants (almost all Western Europeans, such as the Irish and Italians)
1880–1930: New Immigrants (mainly Eastern Europeans, such as Poles, Russians, and other Slavs)
1930–present: Contemporary Immigrants

Students were given the following instructions for the assessments, which covered the remainder of the unit:

For each part of the unit, students will read from several primary sources and work in reading groups to create a presentation dealing with the theme of the American Dream vs. American reality, as it relates to that unit. There are four options for structuring each presentation. It is up to each group to determine which option to exercise for each wave, although no option may be used more than once. The four options include:

- A historical speech (giving a general overview or taking a position for or against immigration)
- A visual project (poster, diorama, or painting)
- A piece of creative writing (poem, letter, diary entry, or interview)
- A skit (4 to 5 minutes long)

Another favorite assignment, with both teachers and students, illustrates how dramatically we changed assessments to reflect our refocused curriculum. As we studied westward expansion, we paid particular attention to government land policy, rampant speculation, and the conditions faced by women on the trail. The original assessment for that unit was for students to create a Western—a fun activity, but one that required a minimal discussion of important content themes. While this assessment was designed to integrate language-arts skills into the curriculum, it did so at the expense of eliminating the social studies content. It also skirted the essential question for the marking period: "What do work and play say about the quality of American life?" That question was the focus of our class discussion, but it was possible to ignore it completely and still write an excellent Western. The following year, we revised the unit. We felt that a valid way to help students understand the issues of both work and play during that period would be to compare and contrast the myth and reality of the old West. We relied on literature, art, and film to present the image of life on the range, while we used primary source accounts, historical texts, and maps to discuss the harsh conditions. The assessment was also revised to ensure that students created a Western narrative that incorporated traditional elements of Western fiction. They were also required to write a companion analytical essay to explain why this myth of the West was more powerful than the reality. We initially were surprised that the students enjoyed writing both pieces. While they appreciated the opportunity to be creative in their Westerns, they also took advantage of the opportunity to discuss what made these fictionalized accounts more appealing. Many students discussed the themes of individuality and the American Dream, the allure of the cowboy, and the draw of the frontier. "The Marlboro man was alive and well in America," one student declared.

Our assessments fostered confidence and competence in the classroom because students believed not only that they were capable of doing the work but also that they had something important to say. This is the hallmark of a competent classroom. It does not mean that the students love to write or that the teachers love to grade; it means that the students appreciate the opportunity to express themselves in an intelligent and meaningful way and that the teachers appreciate the opportunity to see how one line of inquiry can spark so many valid interpretations.

CHAPTER 5

Why Performance Standards?

PROBLEMS WITH POPULAR TECHNIQUES

Our pursuit of a more user-friendly grading system proved to be an exercise in futility until we focused our energy on finding a way to meet our basic need: to communicate to students what they needed to do in order to produce quality work. As we struggled to make two of the more popular techniques, rubrics and assessment checklists, work for us, it became apparent that neither did exactly what we wanted and needed. It was only when we began to experiment with performance standards that we found the concept that worked.

EXPERIMENTS WITH RUBRICS

During the spring of 1996, we tried grading with rubrics, a popular evaluation trend throughout our district. We were instructed by Assistant Superintendent Kuklis that the term *rubric* simply meant any type of scoring system that enables students to succeed more often because they have a better understanding of the characteristics to be included in the finished assessment. In fact, at a rubrics conference we attended, we were taught to define the characteristics of each letter grade for a given assignment so that students could match their performance to the corresponding grade. Through knowing the characteristics of A, B, C, D, and F products, students would gain a deeper appreciation for the impartiality of the grading process and would also be provided with a concrete roadmap to achieve whatever grade level they wished.

We were instantly attracted to the underlying premise: that grading could be correlated to a more objective framework. If writing out the characteristics of each letter grade would enable us to diffuse the tensions grades were producing between students and teachers in our classroom, we were willing to try it. At this stage of our understanding of rubrics, we believed that our students were capable of producing work of a higher quality but were struggling to do so largely because we had poorly communicated our expectations for their work. Rubrics appeared to be the most viable vehicle to dispel the misunderstanding we had with our students about what we expected in a quality product, what they needed to do to meet those requirements, and how the evaluation of what they produced was done in a fair and equitable manner.

Eager to incorporate this new tool into our classroom, we introduced rubrics to our students even though we were in the fourth quarter of the school year. We believed that our students would be flexible enough to adapt to this new approach since we all had so much to gain. The marking period focus was on U.S. wars. Over the span of 10 weeks, we marched chronologically from the American Revolution to the end of the Cold War, allocating approximately 6 class days for each major conflict. Because of the tight time schedule, we thought it would be the ideal time to use rubrics so that we could communicate our expectations for their work in a more effective and efficient manner.

Rubric for a Poem: Explaining Specific Characteristics

Our primary concern was the actual creation of rubrics for each assignment. Although we believed that we intuitively understood the difference between a B thesis statement and a C thesis statement, it was very difficult to explain how they were different without comparing them to one another. Nevertheless, we painstakingly wrote our first several rubrics outlining every significant characteristic of each letter grade. For example, we created a rubric for an assignment that asked students to write a poem describing the patriotic sentiment of colonists during the American Revolution. Our first step was writing a rubric describing what a B poem would look like:

- Demonstrates good understanding of causes of the American Revolution
- Includes at least two reasons why other colonists should join in the fight against the Crown
- Shows patriotic feelings through choice of words and phrases
- Is 25–30 lines long
- Pays attention to the rhythm of language by developing patterns with punctuation, repetition, and/or word sounds
- Has almost no mechanical errors (spelling, punctuation, grammar)
- Is neatly presented (carefully handwritten or typed)

While we completed this step relatively quickly, it took us several hours to write descriptions for the other grades. Our initial concern was how to concretely distinguish the differences for each criterion. We sincerely hoped that the effort would pay off when we presented and implemented the framework in our classroom. The other concern we had was whether or not defining each grade point would send students the wrong message about their achievement on the assessment. By illustrating the difference between an A, a B, and so forth, we were concerned that students would become even more preoccupied with grades. Would some of our students focus on the characteristics of a D poem so that they would know exactly what they could get away with and still pass the course? In other words, did this type of rubric define what quality work looks like or did it explain to students the parameters of the scoring game? Once again, we relied on trial by fire and introduced the rubric to our class.

As we explained the rubric to our students for the first time, their eyes glazed over as we went over each characteristic. We told them that they were now empowered and could "choose" what grade they would receive on the assignment by deciding what level of work they would complete (now that each level was so clearly explained for them).

After we handed students back their patriotic poems graded according to the rubric, one student voiced an important concern, "What happens if you get four characteristics of an A, three of a B, and one of a C? What grade do you get then?" While the question was simple, the answer proved to be much more complicated. By breaking down the various characteristics of a C performance, we had moved beyond holistic scoring. Students would riot if they were given a C unless we could justify how the characteristics were weighted.

Rubric for an Essay: Using General Terms

The next rubric we created was for an essay students were asked to write explaining why the Civil War was the most significant war in American history. Over the course of the unit, we had devoted a considerable amount of time to examining historical and literary documents that described the deep schism that divided the nation. When our students seemed to demonstrate a reasonable comfort level with the materials and key concepts, we introduced the task:

> We have spent a lot of time looking at why other people believe the Civil War would be the turning point in American history. Now it is your turn to articulate your opinion on why "a house divided cannot stand." We want you to write a five-paragraph essay explaining what issues pushed the country into this terrible war. Also, try to wrestle with the idea of whether the war could have been avoided. Could the relationships between blacks and whites be resolved without bloodshed? Think about the relationship between Huck and Jim in

The Adventures of Huckleberry Finn. We know that we are tossing out a lot of different ideas here, but use your rubric to give you a sense of what it will take to earn a good grade on this paper.

The rubric shown in Figure 5.1 did a decent job of delineating what requirements we expected to be incorporated into the assignment, but it also seemed to be a little vague. We were struggling with how concrete to make each characteristic because we found that if we made a characteristic on one grade level very specific, then it was almost impossible for us to describe the same characteristic on the other grade levels. In addition, the first rubric we had created for the patriotic poem on the American Revolution was so assignment-specific that it was not feasible to recycle some of those characteristics into other rubrics. Without the ability to reuse some of the rubric materials, we were sure that this new vehicle was going to require several hours of development time for each assignment. We decided to pilot this more general list of characteristics so that we could refine our rubrics work based on our students' reactions.

Our students once again made little comment when we handed out the rubric to them as we reviewed our expectations for the writing assignment. We encouraged them to use the characteristics as a measuring stick so that they could "aim for the grade" they wanted to receive. Our students' reaction to this rubric taught us two more important lessons. First, we were beginning to realize that rubrics unwittingly encouraged students to identify themselves with specific grading categories. Jane regarded herself as an excellent writer, so she used the "Characteristics of an A paper" as her guide. Frank had much less confidence in his writing and was growing increasingly frustrated with the grades he was earning. Therefore, he decided to take the "easy way out" and just worry about the "Characteristics of a D paper." He believed that rubrics would help him make sure he could pass the class by including the most basic characteristics and thereby investing a minimal amount of effort. When we tried to motivate students, such as Frank, who were aiming for lower grades, they explained that they had always received those grades from teachers.

Bob commented, "Why should I bother to try to be a B-level student when I've earned C grades all year?"

Lauren added, "Rubrics are just telling it like it is. I am a B student and am just kidding myself and wasting my time agonizing over trying to be an A."

The second lesson we learned from our students was that this rubric was indeed too generic. For example, they wanted more concrete numbers to show the difference between a "few" mechanical errors, "some" mechanical errors, and "many" mechanical errors. They wanted to see what writing looked like that was "clear and to the point" and why that characteristic was the

Figure 5.1. Example of a Rubric for an Essay

Characteristics of an A Paper
☞ Typed
☞ Carefully organized
☞ Historically accurate
☞ Clear and to the point
☞ No spelling or grammatical errors
☞ Thought-provoking
☞ Promotes an emotional response (either empathy, anger, sympathy, humor)
☞ Reflects a tremendous amount of effort
☞ Demonstrates strong understanding of class discussions, textbook, and additional materials

Characteristics of a B Paper
☞ Typed or neatly handwritten
☞ Carefully organized into five paragraphs
☞ Historically accurate
☞ Few spelling or grammatical errors
☞ Good concept
☞ Clear and to the point
☞ Demonstrates a significant amount of effort
☞ Incorporates major and minor ideas and materials studied in class

Characteristics of a C Paper
☞ Typed or handwritten
☞ Some thought in organization of the five paragraphs
☞ Somewhat historically accurate
☞ Some spelling or grammatical errors
☞ Good idea, but needed more effort
☞ Incorporates basic ideas and materials studied in class

Characteristics of a D Paper
☞ Handwritten
☞ Many spelling and grammatical errors
☞ Little thought put into organization/not five paragraphs
☞ Not historically accurate
☞ Incorporates few ideas or materials studied in class

Characteristics of an F Paper
☞ Not completed

same on both the A and B levels. They also wanted to understand how we could deduce how much effort they had invested into their work.

Bob complained, "Just because Jane can pull writing out of thin air and make it sound good doesn't mean that the rest of us can do it so easily. I put in a 'tremendous amount of effort.' If you don't believe me, go ahead and call my mom! She was impressed by how hard I worked on it."

We were not pleased with the results of our experiment with this rubric. We had high hopes that we had found a way to make writing rubrics a little less cumbersome by keeping them less specific, but obviously this version did not meet our original objective of finding a better way to articulate to our students our expectations for quality work.

Rubric for a Poster: Averaging Characteristics

The third rubric we designed was for a poster illustrating the need for women to join the work force while American men were fighting overseas in World War II. Carol had painstakingly recreated the image of "Rosie the Riveter," a famous icon that glorified women's new role as munitions workers. Alongside of her illustration, she included key statistics and facts about the impact of these workers on wartime production of necessary materials. The only flaw of the poster was that there were several flagrant spelling errors, including the title of the poster itself. Fred devoted more time to editing his poster, but the images he used to depict women workers were a collage of pictures clipped from the previous week's copy of *Newsweek*. We struggled with how to evaluate these situations equitably. While at first we had done a simple averaging of characteristics, we quickly became dissatisfied with the way grades were turning out. These two students both received higher grades than we thought they deserved, but we did not know how to take off more points without jeopardizing the fairness of the new framework. We decided to continue to average characteristics to see if this issue would get easier as time went on or until we could develop a more equitable system.

Recognizing Problems with Rubrics

In addition to the shades of gray that emerged over this grading issue, our enthusiasm for writing rubrics created more problems. The lengthy rubrics were tiresome to us as well as our students. Even though we were getting more experienced at writing them, we still spent more than 2 hours "perfecting" each one. Not only were we frustrated by the amount of time it took to complete the task; we were even more unhappy about the imperfections that continued to exist in our descriptions of characteristics. It became more expedient to use words like *better* or *more clear* than to actually explain all the qualities of the statement that made it better or more clear (e.g., language was easier to follow, main idea contained a sufficient amount of detail to narrow the focus of the paper). These subjective words, however, weakened the validity of the rubric as students challenged us on defining the difference between *good* and *excellent*. Students began to feel as if we were manipulating the rubric based on our interpretation of whether or not their work was "good." Although we could articulate answers to their challenges, they took several minutes to explain, and they often took place after students had received their grades. Thus, we were again jeopardizing the fairness of the grading process.

Toward the end of the school year, we assigned a take-home essay analyzing the morality of using atomic warfare. We asked students to read an article entitled "The Biggest Decision" and then to evaluate the positive and negative results of President Truman's actions. Weary of writing rubrics and pressed for time, we addressed more specific components of writing an essay than for the Civil War assignment, but our descriptions of characteristics on each grade point remained quite vague. For example, a rubric delineated the student's use of a thesis statement as follows:

> *A Level:* Thesis statement clearly states a position and what topics the student will discuss in order to support his or her idea
> *B Level:* Thesis statement is a little difficult to follow or the topics the student will discuss need to be clarified
> *C Level:* Thesis statement is difficult to follow or the student did not include all topics to be discussed
> *D Level:* Thesis statement or list of topics is not included, creating a weak overall organizational structure for the paper

An examination of Frank's thesis statement for the essay illustrates the problems of using the rubric to grade:

> At the end of World War II, President Harry S. Truman had a tough decision to make. Thank God, he did the right thing or who knows how many more American soldiers would have died. He had a lot of different issues to weigh, both about morality, the nature of war, and the safety of American citizens, but somehow he managed to come up with a decision that would finally make the Japanese give up the fight.

Although Frank had clearly stated his support for President Truman (characteristic of an A), he did not really cover the topics that his paper would include (characteristic of a C). We balanced these differences by giving him a

B for his thesis statement. When Frank received his project grade back graded according to a rubric riddled with subjective phrases, he muttered under his breath, "Thank God for rubrics. Now I know that my work is better than average, but not quite good." We rolled our eyes at each other as he tossed his paper in the wastebasket. We were beginning to resent the time, energy, and issues raised by using rubrics to evaluate our students.

To make matters more difficult, our reluctance to write rubrics cost us one of the key benefits they had added to our classroom: Students were losing their advance notice on how to complete each task successfully. Initially we had handed out the rubric on the same day the actual assignment was given. Even though it took longer to explain both the directions and the grading characteristics, we found that students' comprehension of the requirements for the assignments was much clearer. Because of the time we spent developing the curriculum and the tasks themselves (and because of our frustration), it took longer and longer for us to create the rubrics. We also found the rubrics easier to write as the due date for the assignment approached because we had had the opportunity to see early stages of student work and to further clarify oral and written directions about our vision for the task. Six weeks after we implemented rubrics in our classroom, the day came when a major writing assignment was due and we had never handed out a rubric to our students.

"You promised that we would always have the rubrics first!" Jane complained. Although her essay grades were only a little higher than before we used rubrics, she had become less combative during private sessions on how to improve her writing.

Lauren chimed in, "How do you expect us to be able to do well if you don't tell us what you want us to do?" She had been receiving high marks with the rubrics, just as she had under the more traditional method used earlier in the year, but she liked knowing ahead of time that she had all of the key components for success.

Lessons Learned from Using Rubrics

Once again, we sat down and took stock on the evaluation process and its impact on the relationship between students and teachers. Although we were disappointed with ourselves for failing to complete the rubrics in a timely manner, we also knew that there had to be a more efficient way to create rubrics without sacrificing their integrity. We agreed with our students' complaints about the importance of receiving rubrics earlier, not only because it made sense intellectually but also because of the tangible changes we had seen both in our students' attitudes and in their comprehension of the purpose of the assignment.

We decided to debrief each other about our experience with rubrics at the end of the school year when we had a little more time and could be more objective about the experience. Initially, we were prepared to let rubrics fade away in our memories as another educational reform that could have been good if the potential of the concept could have been carried out in the reality of the classroom. As we began to brainstorm ideas for a different type of rubric format, however, we recognized areas of positive growth from our experiences. First, we appreciated how the rubric sustained our focus during the grading process. Instead of generally surveying a project or a paper and then recording our impressions of the work, we were more attentive to each student's performance in specific skill and content areas. By having the characteristic typed on the page already, our handwritten comments could address the area in more detail. No longer did we wish that we had a rubber stamp that said "be more specific" or "watch your verb tenses" or "what was your source here?" The characteristics made grading student work a more personalized and more rewarding experience for us. Second, the rubrics proved to be a valuable tracking device for student performance. Students were approaching us for help in a specific skill or content area rather than coming to us for more general help. Our discussions were much more productive since the student could better articulate why this area was difficult and we could offer more constructive advice on how to improve his or her performance. Third, fewer students were unhappy with their overall grades. While a number of students asked for explanations as to why they had earned a certain number of grade points for a given characteristic, they seemed more comfortable with the manner in which the evaluation process was conducted. Instead of asking, "Why did you give me this grade?" students now were asking, "Why do I usually not do well on this characteristic?"

In the midst of our self-reflection about the positive and negative lessons we had learned, we suddenly stumbled upon a major revelation. Despite some important gains in the evaluation process, we really had not made a fundamental shift in how we "saw" our students' work. Frank's sarcastic remark about how rubrics just gave him a more detailed explanation of why his work was "better than average but not quite good" was not far off of the mark. Although we had broken down the characteristics of what constitutes a B paper, we still visualized performance holistically. We still knew (and the rubrics reinforced) that Jane's essays were in the low B range because her grammar was not "excellent," her introduction was "fair," and her use of historical sources was almost "good." Jane liked the rubrics not because of our articulation of the characteristics of each grade point, but because there was a list of components that needed to be included in the assignment itself. The rubrics reminded her when she was working on an analytical essay the day before it was due that she needed to write an introduction, use historical sources to prove her ideas, and work on keeping her verb tenses consistent. We had written rubrics that largely validated our own holistic impressions of student work, except now the students better understood that our impressions were based on skill and content issues instead of on where their papers fell on the staircase.

We needed to take a step beyond the traditional rubrics. We recognized that rubrics have a value in that they communicate to students that teachers use rational criteria when evaluating student work. We attempted to improve upon our work with rubrics through the use of assessment checklists, a technique that appeared to be a clearer, more concrete, and more defensible format.

EXPERIMENTS WITH ASSESSMENT CHECKLISTS

Although we never abandoned rubrics as an evaluative tool that year, several of our colleagues had begun to introduce checklists into their classrooms with positive initial results. We understood assessment checklists to be a listing of characteristics that students were expected to include in their work. If we could adopt these checklists as our evaluative tool, we would be able to meet two of our needs that our earlier rubrics had not. First, the checklists seemed to be much easier to create. It seemed that by simply going through the directions for the assignment, we could create a list of all the characteristics we believed should be present in our students' work. Second, the checklists seemed to be more objective. Our students had raised some legitimate concerns about our previous imprecise use of language as we tried to define the difference between the number of points given for each characteristic. Instead of going through the laborious process of defining what grammar, spelling, and punctuation usage looked like for each number of points, we had to define only one criterion that all students were expected to meet. If the students met that expectation, they received the full number of points for that criterion. If the students partially fulfilled that expectation, they would earn some credit, based on how close we believed their work came to meeting the criterion. Total points would then be tallied for an overall grade. To test out the viability of using these checklists in our classroom, we wrote up a sample checklist for the patriotic poem assignment mentioned in the previous section (Figure 5.2).

Although we were sure this system would have kinks that needed to be worked out, we thought our students would be thrilled to have a more black-and-white grading process. The questions suggested by the checklist seemed simpler to us:

Figure 5.2. Assessment Checklist for Patriotic Poem

_____(10 points) Length of poem is 20–30 lines
_____(20 points) Selection of words and phrases illustrates patriotic spirit
_____(20 points) Includes causes of the American Revolution
_____(20 points) Provides reasons why colonists should join the fight against the
                  Crown
_____(10 points) Few mechanical mistakes (spelling, punctuation, grammar)
_____(10 points) Pays attention to the rhythm of language by developing patterns with
                  punctuation, repetition, or word sounds
_____(10 points) Neat presentation of work

- Did you pull details from your sources about the American Revolution?
- Did you put thought into where to end a line and how to punctuate the poem?
- Did you discuss reasons why other colonists should join the fight?

We also felt as if our efforts in creating the checklists were more worthwhile as we devoted our efforts into listing, prioritizing, and weighting different characteristics. While our earlier rubrics had raised questions about how to "average" levels in a consistent manner, we now had the ability to assign point values based on the importance of the skill and content areas.

Term-Paper Checklist

After using assessment checklists for several minor project-based assessments during the first semester, we decided to create a checklist to evaluate the most ambitious task of the school year: the term paper. During the third marking period, students were required to reflect on the connections between a significant piece of American literature and a relevant political or social movement that dominated American life at the time the work was published. They had a minimum of 10 pages to discuss predominant themes in the novel; survey the response of the literary world when the novel was originally published; summarize the major events, figures, and ideas of the political or social movement; and then explain how these areas were interconnected.

Originally, we had spent several afternoons writing a rubric for the final draft of the term paper. That evaluative tool once again attempted to describe the characteristics of each grade level. When we sat down to write the checklist, we pored over both our original rubric and the student directions for the paper. From these, we created a lengthy list of expectations for the final paper in every relevant skill and content area. First, we determined the point values we wanted to assign each component of the paper (which was worth 50 points of the overall term-paper task).

Title Page	2 points
Table of Contents	2 points
Historical Discussion	10 points
Literary Discussion	10 points
Incorporation of Revisions	10 points
Mechanics of Writing	10 points
Works Cited List	6 points

After completing this step, we then wrote a list of characteristics to indicate what the point values were based on. The result was the somewhat cumbersome, but hopefully helpful, checklist shown in Figure 5.3.

Concerns About Using Checklists

Although we were initially pleased by the positive response from our students, when we began to grade the term papers, we became increasingly uncomfortable with each grade we recorded. Two key concerns quickly came the forefront. First, we were concerned that these grades were coming in so low. The term paper constituted 50% of the student's marking period grade, a weighty amount. Because the assessment checklist was very specific, students were penalized for every possible error on their papers. Not surprisingly, many of the grades were low even though the quality of work had improved since their first drafts. Small mistakes were chipping away at the grades of students who had worked hard to include each item on the checklist and who expected their work to pay off when they received their grades.

Second, while we liked the flexibility of being able to attach different point values to each characteristic, we found that we had limited success in doling out partial credit. We struggled to find a fair method of deducting points when the student did make an attempt but still had room to improve.

An example of our predicament was a straightforward item under "Mechanics of Writing"—"MLA format for internal citations for quotations." Sarah cited every quotation, but she placed a comma between the author and the page number (e.g., Hawthorne, 56), an improper use of format. Lauren cited every quotation perfectly, but forgot (or perhaps not) to include citations for two of her quotations in the span of her 12-page paper. Frank provided citations for fewer than half his quotations, and the citations he did write did not follow the MLA format. Under the system we were currently using, Sarah, Lauren, and Frank all received some point deduction on this item. Clearly, none of these students fulfilled the criterion of citing quotations

FIGURE 5.3. Term-Paper Checklist

TITLE PAGE (2 points)
_____ (1 point)   Key information (name, date, class, title)
_____ (1 point)   Organization and layout (typed or neatly handwritten)

TABLE OF CONTENTS (2 points)
_____ (1 point)   Outlines key components of paper and assigns page numbers
_____ (1 point)   Organization and layout (typed or neatly handwritten)

HISTORICAL DISCUSSION (10 points)
_____ (2 points)   4–5 pages in length
_____ (1 points)   Introduction to section states a thesis (what you believe the significance of the historical movement is and impact on American society) and gives an overview of the body paragraphs
_____ (3 points)   Uses supporting details to illustrate ideas (both quotations and facts)
_____ (3 points)   Refers to at least five different sources (only two can be encyclopedias)
_____ (1 point)   Conclusion draws a connection between the historical movement and the novel

LITERARY DISCUSSION (10 points)
_____ (2 points)   4–5 pages in length
_____ (1 point)   Introduction to section states a thesis (one significant theme that you have chosen to discuss through the novel) and gives an overview of the body paragraphs
_____ (2 points)   Uses supporting details and quotations to illustrate ideas
_____ (1 point)   References come from the entire span of the novel
_____ (3 points)   Discussion of literary criticism about the novel when it was published
_____ (1 point)   Conclusion draws a connection between the novel and its literary critics

INCORPORATION OF REVISIONS (10 points)
_____ (3 points)   Content changes to historical discussion
_____ (3 points)   Content changes to literary discussion
_____ (2 points)   Overall mechanical changes
_____ (2 points)   Note from the author outlining revisions included in the final draft

MECHANICS OF WRITING (10 points)
_____ (1 point)   Topic sentences
_____ (1 point)   Transitions
_____ (2 points)   MLA format for internal citations for quotations
_____ (2 points)   Use of punctuation
_____ (2 points)   Use of grammar
_____ (2 points)   Spelling

WORKS CITED LIST (6 points)
_____ (2 points)   Entries presented in alphabetical order
_____ (4 points)   Use of MLA format for full entries

correctly. At this point the clarity ended for us. It was difficult to assign point value difference that distinguished between those students who almost got it right from those students who barely made an attempt.

A third concern was that we did not believe that the checklists provided a holistic assessment of the term papers. Some students had bent over backward to include every item on the checklist. The results of these exhaustive efforts were relatively high marks. Some students read through the checklist but decided to focus more on the overall paper rather than the detailed characteristics. The unintentional result was that students whose learning styles were "concrete and sequential" thrived with the checklist and those whose styles were "abstract and random" were sorely disappointed. Although we believed all students must be accountable for the components that constitute a quality term paper, we also believed that there was an overall concept of quality that we had failed to include in our evaluation tool. The result was that students who wrote mechanically strong but intellectually uninspired papers were earning higher grades than the students who produced powerful insights but struggled with the organization of their ideas.

Everyone was unhappy the next day when we returned the final drafts. Sarah and Lauren complained bitterly that their minor mistakes had cost them so much. Our students were remarkably deft at discovering what marks their peers received in each area—a practice that tests the consistency of the grading process as well as the good humor of their teachers—and it soon became clear to many of them that those students who had worked halfheartedly on their last draft fared almost as well as those who had invested substantial effort in the endeavor. The old complaint from the first semester of the school year—"Do you really expect us to work hard in here if we know that we are not going to do well?"—haunted our classroom that day.

Evaluating Checklists

While the checklist clearly delineated our expectations of student work on the term paper, it left us with little leeway to distinguish different degrees of success in each area. Although the black-and-white nature of the checklist made our grading more objective, it also made it less fair. The benefit of being able to concretely evaluate whether or not a thesis statement existed came at the cost of evaluating the quality of the statement itself. While we created a separate category to address the overall quality and clarity of the students' writing, the checklist fragmented the paper into too many separate parts whose sum did not seem to equal the whole. For the first time, there was a serious divergence between our holistic impression of students' performances and the grades that they actually received. The grading structure had pulled us back into a scoring game in which it seemed that students were negotiating for a different interpretation of a checklist item rather than focusing on the more meaningful goal of raising their achievement level. We were growing more and more impatient with the triviality of our discussions with students about grades. Both the assessment checklists and our definitions of work on each grade level may have improved our students' advance understanding of what was expected from them, but we still remained bogged down by their bottom line mentality of "so what's my grade?"

Although we briefly discussed asking the school administration to revolutionize the evaluation process by eliminating numerical grades completely, we were determined to find a solution to the difficulties of evaluating student work. Assessment checklists brought us one substantial step closer to our goals, but they still fell short of our expectations. We believed that we could find a better balance between our idealistic visions of having students produce quality work with our pragmatic concerns about assigning reasonable point values to those achievements. A year's work with both rubrics and assessment checklists left us unsatisfied. Each had advantages, but neither was the answer we were seeking.

PERFORMANCE STANDARDS: THE EXPERIMENT WORKS

Performance standards proved to be the evaluative concept we had been searching for. Our use of these standards was based on the premise that all students could improve their performance in the classroom if they understood what was expected from them in advance. While this premise may sound similar to the one that underlay our work with rubrics, the key difference here was that the performance standard became the goal. A performance standard is an objective sentence articulating a specific content area or skill focus we expected the students' work to demonstrate. The standards list breaks down the elements of work into simple, concrete, and specific units that the students can understand more easily and that teachers and students can discuss intelligently without making blanket generalizations about the work. When our students received performance standards regularly and consistently in advance of their assignments, their work changed both qualitatively and quantitatively. We already knew how using standards had changed us as teachers; the real revolution was how a standards-based curriculum changed students.

Improved Communication

One of the most meaningful lessons we learned from our work with performance standards was that they were an excellent way to improve communication and build trust between the student and the teacher. When performance standards were handed out to students with an assignment, they engaged that student in a contract with the teacher: If you agree to include these criteria in your performance, you will be successful. Because we were confident that we could create good standards in a timely fashion, we committed to our students (and to ourselves) that we would never assign a performance task without also providing a list of performance standards. Although this resolution was not always easy to keep, it was an essential part of our success. Glasser (1986) has pointed out that curriculum work such as ours goes far beyond tinkering with educational language because we are "structuring our whole approach in a way that [students] want to work to learn" (p. 79). We were reminded that if understanding the grading expectations ahead of time makes students believe that they have a better chance of being successful and completing more meaningful work, we had an absolute duty to provide that information to them. We had always wanted to give our students this information, but up until this point, the communication had been somewhat muddled for one of three reasons: we articulated our expectations clearly through oral directions that made students feel confident about their understanding until they were home alone facing a blank computer screen; we wrote down what our expectations were with minimal detail or explanation about what constituted a good thesis statement or weak use of sources; or we gave detailed feedback about our expectations when we returned their work to them. We used different samples of student work to demonstrate how well they had met our expectations. Although we believed that these discussions would help to improve their understanding of how we graded, in fact our students were much more resistant to constructive criticism if the evaluations were already completed. By providing performance standards for every assessment in advance, we were providing more information about our expectations as to what the finished product should look like at the start of an assignment.

We found that using performance standards eliminated a significant amount of subjectivity from the grading process that had been present in assessment checklists. For example, when we first assigned a project in which students were asked to make a collage of one of the new cultural trends of the "Roaring Twenties," we used the following assessment checklist to evaluate the final product.

    _____   House Set Variety of images (30 points)
    _____   Historical representation of topic (30 points)
    _____   Presentation of images and information (30 points)
    _____   Overall effort (10 points)

While the characteristics we valued in the collage were clear, it remained a mystery to students how we attributed points to those characteristics. What was the difference between a 25 and a 27 for variety of images? What did a 26 look like? The same assignment was given the next year, but this time with performance standards.

- The student's collage contains a minimum of five images.
- The student selects images that are historically representative of the time period.
- The student presents the clippings of images and information in a manner that is accessible from a short distance away from the collage.
- The student uses class time effectively to complete the task.

This version much more clearly established the standards expected in every student's work.

How Students Benefit

Our students' experiences working with performance standards provided them with two important experiences. After a year of working with them, American Studies students had more faith in their academic competence. More important, they demonstrated this competence in the work that they produced.

First, students felt more in control of their performance in American Studies. The "big picture" that we had created for the course was new. We made serious headway in demystifying the learning process for them by structuring the course around a few clear, coherent essential questions that represented our content standards. Moreover, each and every task was integrated into that "big picture," and the performance standards broke the task down into manageable, comprehensive pieces. When Leah or Claire sat down to write an essay, each had a list before her that told her clearly what her teachers valued in the assignment and what she needed to do to meet the standard. From that point on, meeting standard became easier for many students. Leah commented on one self-evaluation form, "Performance standards tell you what the teachers want, and you just have to put in the effort for a good grade." An oversimplification, to be sure, but the student who wrote that line believed that success was within her grasp because she understood the process necessary to earn the grade. It was an extremely positive step for an eleventh-grader who routinely said, "She gave me the grade" to talk in terms of "much more responsibility: I can choose my own grade based on my effort." Of course, it did not mean writing the grade of choice at the top of the paper, but when the course could be explained as a unified whole, when every part fit with and made sense in terms of every other part, then it became easier to focus on expectations and to rise to meet them.

If the process stopped there, however, we would have had little to write about. Instead, the good news is that the quality of student performance rose steadily as the year progressed.

Our students needed the focus of knowing the most important aspects of the assignment, what arbitrary numbers we determined as standard, and what it was worth to them to meet that standard. Our values created the standards; their internalizing and practicing those values (e.g., writing a thesis statement or using supportive details) automatically improved their performance. As Robert put it, "Some of the performance standards stay the same, so I can ace those and practice on the new ones. Each time I write, I know a little bit more." It is not just that students feel they have more control; students become more competent because they truly do have more control over their success in the classroom.

Most adults agree that learning, like any other worthwhile activity, demands hard work. Out of that hard work comes constant but gradual improvement. Trying to convince eleventh-graders that they want to work harder is more of a struggle. The standards-based curriculum of American Studies did, however, convince many of our students to do extra work, mainly in the form of revision. Most teachers who allow or encourage revision of work tend to become discouraged. They spend hours annotating work, making corrections, writing suggestions and comments. Then, when the student submits a revision, the changes are often minimal. Larger, more time-consuming issues of thought and organization are rarely addressed; the spell-checking function on a computer cannot read for appropriateness of word choice; and the student has not bothered to reread his or her own work. Nevertheless, the student expects (and perhaps demands) a higher grade, because "I did it over; I did so much more work."

Performance standards provide the common language for teachers and students to share their mutual expectations. The set of performance standards used to evaluate a paired writing debate on the impact of Reconstruction on the rights of African Americans, for example, informed students of exactly what was expected from them.

- The student is on-task throughout the activity, using the assigned class time to prepare and to write his or her assigned position on Reconstruction.
- The student clearly and persuasively articulates reasons for why his or her interpretation of Reconstruction is the most valid.
- The student uses specific historical support from the reading packet to support his or her arguments.

- The student directly responds to the questions and comments made by his or her paired writing partner.

Revision did not mean throwing out the graded copy and starting over again. It could be as simple a task as adding more supportive details to illustrate one of the arguments against the Reconstruction program or including more direct responses to his or her partner's comments. "If you have a problem with the paper, it is so much easier to discuss it with the performance standards," wrote Roger, echoing the fact that students revised more (and more often) when they had specific target areas. In addition, they were not tempted to discard what was good about the paper, because the standards indicated to the students what was competent or exemplary about their work. For Robert, that was an encouragement. He wrote, "I like this because it not only shows me where I made mistakes, but also where I have excelled, and this made me feel good."

Our students invested more in our course now because they got more out of it. Convinced that they were treated fairly and were trusted with the crucial knowledge of how to be successful in our classroom, they responded by taking responsibility for their actions and by doing more work. The further reward was that the students' work improved, raising their skill level and self-confidence.

The Difficulty of Assigning Grades

How are performance standards tied to grades? Performance standards inform students about how to produce quality work. As they began to adopt the standards as a measuring stick for their performance, they began to think less in terms of numerical grades and more in terms of meeting or exceeding standard. This more enlightened perception of grades, however, would dissipate as soon as they received their work back. Once again, they resumed the search for the number that would indicate to them their level of success. Only after seeing that grade would they pause and reflect on how they earned that grade—where they exceeded, met, and fell below standard. The result was that our students operated in a fragmented world where the curriculum demands quality thought, the assessments provide them the opportunity to showcase their quality understanding, the performance standards affirm the quality of the finished product . . . and the numerical grades continue to represent their efforts.

We therefore were faced with a troubling dilemma: Do numerical grades distort the meaning of standards? The unfortunate, but practical, response was "yes." While we could instinctively identify quality work, we continued to wrestle with assigning numbers with some modicum of fairness. We were not so revolutionary as to suggest to our administrators that the district should abandon the numerical grading system in favor of a standards-based vision. While some critical friends have faulted us for not following through on this logical extension of our work, we had chosen at this point in our careers to change only that over which we had immediate control. Therefore, in order to play the grading game, we manipulated our performance standards system to translate into numerical grades, as we explain in Chapter 6.

In order to inform parents of how our classroom system was working, we opted not to use the high school Scantron progress reports and instead took the time to write parents more meaningful, more personalized comments about the quality of their son's or daughter's performance at the midpoint of each marking period. Then, at the end of each quarter, we mailed home a grading sheet listing all the grades that student received, along with handwritten comments in order to explain to parents what the numerical grade meant for their particular child. We encouraged students who were trying to improve their grades to keep their eyes fixed on the standards instead of the number at the bottom of the page. This application of performance standards has been our last, best attempt to teach our students to pursue quality work within the evaluation structure used by almost every public school district in the United States. While it may still be an imperfect attempt to rectify an imperfect situation, it reformed our evaluation system from within by creating a reasonable, effective, and meaningful evaluation process that both teachers and students could believe in.

CHAPTER 6

How Are Performance Standards Used to Calculate Grades?

PLAYING THE NUMBERS GAME IN THE MOST PALATABLE WAY

To align our philosophical love for performance standards with our practical dilemma of assigning numerical grades, we devised a points system that would reward students for producing quality work. The common "bar" that every student was expected to be able to hurdle was not achieving a number or a letter, but meeting standard. While this may sound more like wordsmithing than meaningful reform, this paradigm shift radically altered the parameters of what doing well looked like in our classroom. Although parents, administrators, and guidance counselors perceived that a 65 or higher was "passing" in our classroom, our students could no longer operate from that perspective. Similar to the self-pigeonholing that took place with rubrics, once again students had to choose the level of performance they would invest in their work. The difference this time, however, was that this level was no longer defined by a letter or number; it was a fundamental choice about whether or not they would meet the expectations of the class. It was impossible for students to opt to "just get by"—they could either fall below standard, meet standard, or exceed standard.

CREATING STANDARDS FOR ASSESSMENTS

To establish the grading mechanism for a given assessment, we would first construct a list of performance standards by extracting the vital elements from the directions for the assessment (see Appendix B for more information on creating performance standards). Every performance standard on the list needed to state what in the students' performance demonstrated mastery of the task. For example, if we asked students to include a variety of source materials, our standard would explain that expectation:

- The student uses a minimum of three primary and secondary sources to support his or her ideas.

The focus of the tool became assessing whether or not the student's work met our expectations in each area. If a student met standard, he or she received a "check" on the grading sheet next to the statement of the standard. We explained to our students that a "check" meant that the sentence (or expectation) held true for their work. Having all the standards typed out on the grading sheet meant that we did not have to write the same comments over and over and over again on students' assignments when they met standard. If the student exceeded or fell below our expectations, we would indicate that with a "plus" or "minus," respectively, and indicate in writing concrete reasons for that evaluation.

After creating a list of 5 to 10 performance standards for a task, the next step was to associate point values with the evaluation tool. Because the standards articulated our expectations for quality work, we decided to establish a numerical grade in the B range for assessments meeting standard, or receiving checks for all standards of the task. We believe that because our standards are rigorous, those students who meet those academic goals are not "just getting by" but are successful. We are firmly convinced that this is not grade inflation, but rather raising the bar of expectations for all students. However, we have come to accept that this methodology does not work for all teachers. We have heard many passionate arguments from teachers who believe that standard has to be a C. Certainly standard can be established in the C range, but in our opinion the message then is that "average" is good enough. This evaluation tool can work effectively with both numerical grade bases, although we continue to believe that students will rise to the level of expectation wherever the bar is placed.

Having decided that meeting standard would earn a grade in the B range for each assignment, we had to determine what the specific numerical grade would be and how many points a check plus and a check minus would be worth. We decided to select a number for standard so that it would be mathematically possible for students to earn 100 points if they earned a check plus for all the performance standards. That is, to make the math easy for ourselves, we vary the number in the B range at which we set standard so that the check plus will be a whole number (decimals are an unnecessary hassle). To illustrate:

- If a task has 5 performance standards, meeting standard (or receiving a check for each standard) earns 85 points. In this task, each check plus is worth 3 points. Receiving a check plus on all 5 standards gains 15 points over standard (85) for a score of 100.
- If a task has 8 performance standards, the total points earned when meeting standard is an 84. Each check plus equals 2 points. In this

case earning all check pluses is worth 16 points, which added to 84 results in a score of 100.

Then we had to determine how low a student's grade could go if he or she completed the assignment but receives a check minus for every standard. Our experiments in this area have led us to assign the same number of points to a check plus and a check minus. Our students expressed moral outrage when a check-minus deduction was double or triple the number of points possible for a check plus. While we did follow their advice in this area, we also introduced the concept of zero (as explained later in this chapter) to distinguish between a student who was working toward standard and a student who did not make a good-faith attempt to meet the performance standard. A zero is an automatic 10-point deduction from the overall grade. The zero is necessary to indicate the difference between trying to meet a requirement but falling short and not expending the effort. For example, if a standard requires that students write a thesis statement in the introduction that provides an overall focus for the discussion of a topic, there should be a difference in points between a student who writes a poor thesis statement and a student who does not write a thesis statement at all.

Again, while this system has worked well for us, other teachers are more comfortable assigning higher point deductions for a check minus than a check plus. We have found that the key is communicating the point assignments to the students ahead of time so that they clearly know how grades will be calculated. For teachers who want to change the number of points depending upon the significance of the performance standard, we strongly recommend that the points for the check plus and check minus be written next to each performance standard to avoid any confusion.

Once numerical points have been assigned to ensure that a student can earn 100 if he or she receives all check pluses, the evaluation tool is complete. When using the tool to score papers, we evaluate the student work one standard at a time. If a student receives a check plus, a check minus, or a zero, we indicate to the student in writing beneath the standard the reason for our evaluation. This helps the student understand the strengths and weaknesses of his or her performance, especially if there is an opportunity to revise work. After evaluating the student on each standard, we then calculate the total score by starting at the number that standard is set at (in the B range) and adding or subtracting from that point.

To illustrate how performance standards are used to evaluate student work, in Figure 6.1 we present an assessment on World War I. Included in the figure are the essential question for the unit, the directions for the as-

Figure 6.1. Sample Student Assessment: Letter to the Editor on World War I

Essential Question
Are we in it for the money?

Directions
You will have approximately 45 minutes to complete a draft of a letter to the editor. Use this letter as a vehicle to express your reaction to an article written on World War I. Although you do not need to prepare in advance for this activity, you must have all related unit materials with you so that you can respond in an intelligent and comprehensive manner. The tone of the letter is highly personal. It is your reaction to the presentation of events. (Yes, you can use the word *I*.)

Student Sample

HARD KNOCK LIFE
        Your article in the newspaper last week on trench warfare was very informative. I feel as if I was there experiencing those conditions that you so strongly described. Even though parts were a bit graphic, I enjoyed reading about what is going on out there. It is important that we, the citizens, know what our men and boys are enduring in the trenches. I believe you deserve much recognition for letting America know about the unsanitary conditions, the rats, the illnesses, and all the other "horrible conditions of hell." The description of the rats in the article was very vivid and disgusting, but I can't blame you for revealing the truth. "The rats were huge. They were so big they would eat a wounded man if he couldn't defend himself." I have heard of rats the size of dogs before but no one has ever described them so strongly. I can't imagine being surrounded by dead bodies everywhere. "We set to work to try and drain it. Our efforts were hampered by the fact that the French, who had first occupied it, had buried their dead in the bottom and sides. Every stroke of the pick encountered a body. The smell was awful." It must have been unimaginable for those men surrounded by dead bodies. "The stench of the dead bodies now is awful as they have been exposed to the sun for several days, many have swollen and burst."
        Making a story realistic is most important. I believe you have done an adequate job of using descriptive words, quotes, and phrases to define every detail to make it even more realistic. It is so difficult for those outside the war to imagine the conditions inside of the war. I believe your article brings attention to the actual conditions. You deserve all the credit for presenting America with all the gruesome details possible to bring trench warfare to a reality, for those non-believers. Thank you for the truth.

John Doe
123 My Street
Newtown, CT

(*continued*)

PERFORMANCE STANDARDS

Standard is set at an 86. A check plus = +2, a check minus = −2. A zero (−10 points) will be given if the student does not make a good-faith attempt to meet standard.

√−   1. The student organizes the content of the letter in an authentic format.

While the basic format is good, your ideas should be broken down into smaller paragraphs.

√   2. The student articulates a purpose for writing the letter.

A nice compliment, but how did the information compel your response?

√   3. The student uses words and phrases to persuade readers to ascribe to his/her perspective.

Good start—another key part of persuasion is your incorporation of details.

√−   4. The student showcases his/her knowledge about the World War I topic.

You still need to establish broader understanding of WWI.

√+   5. The student addresses the factual information and perspective presented in the assigned article.

Very good balance of positive and negative points. You clearly reflected on the article.

√−   6. The student offers additional historical and/or literary details either to contradict or to enhance the presentation of information in the article.

Continue to add in more information to support your ideas.

√   7. The student proofreads his/her letter to eliminate mechanical errors.

A few errors, but primarily need to work on sentence structure.

Name: John Doe Grade: 82
> *Calculation Method:* Standard = 86 (7 performance standards,
> check plus = +2, check minus = −2).
> Grades = 3 checks, 1 check plus, 3 check minuses
> 86 . . . 86 + (1 × 2) = 88 . . . 88 − (3 × 2) = 82.
> **GRADE = 82**

sessment, a student's essay, the evaluation sheet, and our calculations of the grade. See Appendix B for an additional example.

REVISING THE USE OF STANDARDS

After several months of standards work, the evaluation tool became more user-friendly to the students as they became reassured by the reappearance of standards by which they had been evaluated before. This familiarity not only made them feel as if they had a better chance of being successful but also gave us valuable training in consistency in interpretation and application of standards.

As demonstrated in Chapter 5, performance standards proved to be a vast improvement over any other grading system we had implemented. Yet with the use of standards, several issues emerged: what to do when we forgot to include a standard, how to handle a standard that was too ambiguous or subjective, how to handle the evolution of our own standards work, and how to improve our calculation of grades using standards. We knew that each of these issues needed to be resolved or we would jeopardize our contract with students that guaranteed the rules of the game before the students played.

Correcting Omissions

As we worked to establish our expectations for each performance task, there were instances throughout the year when we forgot to include a standard for a certain content area or skill focus. These oversights quickly became clear to us when we used the standards to evaluate students' work. Our experience with assigning an essay on the influence of Puritanism on American life illustrates the problem. When we wrote the standards, we brainstormed every conceivable value of the assignment that we wanted to include in our assessment tool, from historical accuracy to demonstration of understanding of poems we had discussed in class to proofreading for grammatical mistakes. It was not until we began to grade the essays that we made a startling discovery: We had no standard that held students accountable for the organization of their ideas. Consequently, we received four essays in the form of one long paragraph that spanned two to three pages. These paragraphs were grammatically accurate, historically responsible, and full of poetic references, but the organization of ideas was nonexistent. Although we really wanted to penalize the students for not structuring an overall argument, we remembered our promise to maintain the integrity of the standards once work on the assignment had begun. We asked ourselves whether it was worth sacrificing our contract with students never to change the standards in order to lower the grades of these four students. We have remained faithful to our answer to this question every day since this roadblock first appeared: If we forgot to include a performance standard, we were accountable for the omission, not the students. We informed our students the next day, saying, "You got lucky, but beware: For the next assignment, you will need to write those topic sentences. There will be a standard." The key here, however, was to remain vigilant about revising the standards immediately after we finished grading students' work.

Clarifying Language

For some assessments, the language used in the standards made sense to us but was unclear to our students. Whether the language was muddled or came across too subjectively, our students were quick to challenge the validity of a weak standard. An example of a standard needing improvement was one of the first ones we ever wrote: "The student's writing is smooth, flowing, and easy to follow." The value behind the standard was clear to us: We were looking for papers that read like a smooth ride instead of like a student learning to drive a standard-shift car for the first time. The language used to express the value, however, was shaky at best. We were immediately alerted to the problem when one student raised her hand and inquired, "What does flowing language look like?" At first we responded with more metaphors and similar phrases, but we noticed that she still looked puzzled. Finally, we began to explain about transitions, topic sentences, and writing an essay that has more than one long paragraph, and the student began to nod her head in understanding. Once again, it was clear to us that communication was the key; if our students understood the standards, they were more likely to succeed. We found that our students would forgive glitches along the way as long as we listened to their questions and concerns about what the standard was requiring and honored our agreement not to change the language of the standards once they began to work on the assignment.

Checking Standards' Alignment with Assessments

We learned the hard way that our performance standards evolved over the course of our work. Although we believe in the benefits of reusing standards on different assessments, this practice worked only when our vision for the assessment remained constant. An example of the negative ramifications of recycling old standards was a project on cultural revolutions of the Roaring Twenties. Two of the previous year's standards had read:

- The student includes examples from class readings as supportive detail.
- The student's project demonstrates thought and preparation.

While we had revised performance standards for the assignment over the summer (just 4 months earlier), we forgot that the first standard originally required only class readings because of the limited availability of the school's library media center that year because of construction work. However, we now had full access to the center and provided students with the opportunity to research their topics during class time. Failure to revise this first standard resulted in a weaker level of accountability for student research. The second standard presented another fundamental problem; it was no longer in sync with our realization that we could not explain how we judged thought and preparation. Both standards were too vague, and, of course, our hopes of concealing our blunder were squashed as students fiercely complained about the fairness of the assessment tool.

"The standard said that I needed to demonstrate thought in the presentation. Do you have a clue on how hard I thought about this project? It gave me a headache I thought so hard!"

"How can you say that I don't have enough historical support in my project? I have two facts from the reading packets you gave us. You never said how much historical support you wanted!"

Our attempt to change the parameters of the assignment without changing the performance standards backfired because we had broken our own rules. Performance standards have to align exactly with assignments. Shortcuts proved both foolhardy and frustrating in terms of the goodwill we were attempting to build. This experience reinforced the fact that we must remain vigilant in ensuring that our standards are in alignment with the particular task. We knew from past experience that we could assign the same performance assessment 2 years in a row and have different expectations of our students about what that performance should look like because of the class personality, the unpredictable direction of class discussions, and current topics that immediately impact the curriculum. We found it necessary to tailor the performance standards to both the demands of the assignment and the character of the class. Among all the variables that the average classroom presented, we needed to put in place the constant that each and every performance standard would be carefully aligned with its corresponding assessment in order to ensure that we communicated our values clearly to our students.

Refining the Grading Connection

Through our experience with using standards, we diagnosed a problem with the way we were associating numerical values with our evaluation of student performance on assessments. As explained earlier, our original structure was to set standard in the B range. Our standards-based assignments were founded on the premise that to meet standard required good, not average, work. We would not consider listing standard as the barely passing D or the "gentleman's C." We also wanted to ease our students' preoccupation with numbers and instead fix their sights on meeting (and exceeding) the goals of the task at hand. Mathematically, that left little space between the standard grade and 100, but tons of room between standard and zero. Almost invariably, we made a check minus cost twice as many points as a check plus. Still, unless there were 10 or more standards, the lowest grade a student could earn would be 50 points or better.

We found ourselves more and more frequently splitting the difference and awarding a check–check plus or a check–check minus. A standard that read "the student incorporates evidence from reading, lecture, discussion, and film into his or her paper" would earn a check–check minus if the student used three of the four sources listed or used all four sources, but not very effectively, or displayed uneven quality by using some sources well and some not. We wanted students to know that it was possible that some of the values in the standard had been met, while others had not. When conducting workshops on performance standards for our colleagues, we rationalized this "splitting the difference" approach on the grounds that sometimes the student deserved half credit because he or she "almost" met standard.

It was not until the summer that we realized the intellectual cost of this straddling-the-fence approach. Although we were trying to spare our students' feelings and grades by awarding partial credit, instead we were undermining the success of our standards work. Once we started doling out partial credit, we also started receiving more complaints about why some students received partial credit while others did not. More importantly, we realized that it was difficult to consistently give partial credit . . . we knew in our hearts that we were influenced by everything from how hard a student was trying, to the level of improvement in that area over the course of the year, to the personality of the student. In addition to avoiding these subjective pitfalls, we did not want to dilute the powerful message of the standards concept. This tool was so effective because of its concreteness and its objectivity: Either the student met standard, exceeded standard, or fell below standard.

To strengthen the fairness and integrity of our application of performance standards, we decided to take three concrete actions. First, we would keep our sympathies in check and preserve the integrity and importance of achieving standard. Second, we would revise standards where we found ourselves "splitting the difference" to ensure that there was only one value students were asked to meet. Third, we would introduce the concept of zero to indicate the difference between the student who attempts to meet a given standard and falls short versus the student who does not try to meet the standard at all.

Our first major change was primarily a philosophical shift about how we treated our standards during the grading process. We believed above all else that the integrity of the standards had to be maintained and that our tendency to give partial credit was undermining our work. We had been "splitting the difference" to come up with the right "numerical grade," not because we believed in the validity of giving partial credit. In order to remain loyal to our philosophical shift, however, we needed to implement two more changes to our vision of performance standards as an evaluative tool.

Our second major change was to limit each standard to one primary focus, instead of compiling several different values into one evaluative sentence. By creating two separate standards out of the one sentence, we hoped to indicate to our students that both aspects were important to us. Part of the reason we had awarded partial credit was to attempt to balance our holistic view of the work with the individual standard that did not say enough (or said too much). Mentally, we had been looking for another standard to grade, and since it was not there, we used a check–check plus or a check–check minus to indicate our discomfort. It goes without saying that we will continue to take a hard look at such standards. Our aim is clarity; we have to be sure that we say exactly what we mean.

In addition to the issue of partial credit, another long-term grading concern was the number of points students were given for below-standard work. Again, standard was set in the 84–88 range depending on the number of standards for the task. On average we used between five and nine standards for a given evaluation tool. The penalty, therefore, for a check minus would be astronomical if we tried to go from a B range to a zero. Consequently, we had deducted double the number of points a student would earn for a check plus so that the student would bottom out at anywhere from a 50 to a 65. What did that mean for a student who submitted a task with one or more significant components of the assignment missing? What if the standard read, "The student cites sources correctly"? A student who incorporated an appropriate number of sources, but cited them incorrectly, would earn a check minus. A student who incorporated no sources at all would also earn a check minus for the same standard without expending any effort at all. We were extremely uncomfortable with the message that this sent to both students. Why bother trying to complete a difficult standard if trying and failing is graded the same as not trying at all? The student who cited the sources incorrectly got a negative message about fairness, and both learned how to beat the system. In the same way, the standard "The student's thesis statement organizes and directs the discussions of the entire paper" can also become a teacher trap. Should it cost the same number of points to formulate a thesis statement badly as not to do it at all? In retrospect, this problem helps to explain a bit more how we fell into the habit of using the check–check minus on so many papers. We wanted to save the real minuses for those students who had completely failed to meet standard.

To solve this problem, our third and final change was to incorporate the concept of zero into our grading system to indicate that the student's work did not demonstrate a meaningful attempt at meeting standard in a given area. A zero would result in a standard deduction of 10 points: a costly omission, but a strong indication to students to try to pay more attention to their list of standards and incorporate each one into their work. Although this approach initially felt a little harsh, we believed that it would eliminate a grading loophole that had been exploited (intentionally and unintentionally). Student responses indicated that the standards system worked for them. Our job then was to make it work better, which meant more fairly, more concretely, more objectively, and more honestly. Ideally, by using performance standards, we have eliminated the little groups in the corner of the classroom buzzing about who got away with what: "Well Peter never even went to the library for sources for his research paper and he got a check minus! I spent all day Sunday there and because my format was a little funny, I got a check minus, too! Why bother?" Although none of our students appreciated the loss of 10 points, they rarely argued when they received (or gave themselves) the mark. Generally, students earned a zero on a standard because they simply "forgot" to include the requirement or they "didn't have the time to get around to it."

The changes we made to improve our evaluation system continued to reinforce the concept that the use of performance standards was a contract for quality work between teachers and students to be honored equally on both sides and revised when necessary.

GAINS FOR STUDENTS AND TEACHERS

This system revolutionized how our students saw themselves as performers. For example, instead of Crystal thinking of herself as a B– writer, she now has a completely different focus—meeting or exceeding standard for each content area and skill focus. Although this grading system did not eliminate student complaints about grades, it ensured that any conversations about the evaluation were focused on specific issues rather than personality conflicts. Not only did performance standards improve student performance, but they also enabled us to become more successful evaluators. While we had struggled to create good rubrics in a relatively timely fashion, we found that, despite the time spent, they still did not communicate what we valued to our students.

One example illustrating the difference between rubrics and performance standards was our effort to articulate what public-speaking elements are necessary for an effective oral presentation. When we first began experimenting with rubrics, we established what an A on delivery of an oral presentation would look like:

- The student engages audience attention, makes frequent and sustained eye contact with the audience, varies volume and inflection, and displays a high energy level.

Our students had dutifully read the rubric, but they were puzzled about the difference between earning an A and a B since the language for the B delivery appeared to be virtually identical.

When we developed a performance standard for the delivery of an oral presentation, our values remained the same as those in our earlier rubric. The standard, however, communicates our expectation for all students in the class:

- The student establishes a connection with his or her audience through the use of eye contact, volume, inflection, and energy level.

Any students who exceeded standard demonstrated a higher proficiency of public speaking, whereas any students who fell below standard demonstrated that they needed to continue to develop their delivery skills in order to meet one of the goals of the course. When we created a common standard instead of trying to define delivery of an oral presentation at each grade level, our students still had a clear understanding of what was expected from them, as they had had with rubrics. However, no longer were they asked to identify themselves with a specific grade. Instead of shooting for a B or just trying to squeak through with a passing grade, our students now had to choose either to meet the goal, exceed the goal, or fall short of the goal.

When we gave this assignment, we first explained and modeled to our students how the aspects listed in the performance standard help the speaker to establish a connection with the audience. Then, our students worked on their oral presentations. When it came time for the students to give their talks, we asked for volunteers to complete the performance standards grading sheet as one of their peers delivered an oral presentation. This was the first year of our working together with performance standards, and we had not previously experimented at all with student self-evaluation, which we discuss further in Chapter 7. Finally, Roger reluctantly raised his hand. Our students seemed uncomfortable evaluating someone else's work either because they were not sure how to be objective or because they believed that they were not experienced enough as evaluators to determine a reasonable grade. Generally, students regarded peer evaluations as glorified popularity contests or mundane exercises that were forced upon them. Roger sat down next to us and dutifully listened to our reminders about how grading with standards worked. As the first presenter began to speak, Roger started to place marks next to the standards. Toward the end of the presentation, he readjusted two of his marks and then began to write comments down explaining how he determined the grade. He smiled when he saw that his evaluation was almost identical to ours. After listening to about 10 more of his peers, Roger turned to us and whispered, "Can I do my oral presentation over again? I really understand what I have to do now." Because ownership of performance standards lies in helping students to understand each expectation, students performed better as they became more accustomed to the standard. Roger, who redid his oral presentation, carried his new understanding of what elements ensure a successful delivery into future presentations throughout the remainder of the course. We still had a long way to go in incorporating student evaluations of their own and their peers' work into our curriculum, but the exercise helped many students understand the standards better.

The dramatic effects of the paradigm shift can be seen specifically in three areas of student perception: their ideas about the fairness of the curriculum, their feelings of growing competency, and their willingness to work. We owe a good deal of our success to the fact that after a breaking-in period in which we all got used to using performance standards, students could see how fairly and objectively they were treated. Every teacher can recall uncomfortable confrontations with students after a paper is graded. "You just don't like me" usually comes at the end of a litany of complaints, including "Well, Tara got a better grade than I did, and I worked just as hard" or "Tara got a better grade, but I don't see any difference in our work." By providing performance standards when a task was first introduced and by addressing any student concerns about language and expectations, we then shifted accountability for success to the students. One of our students said it best: "I choose how well I want to do because I already know what is expected from me. I just have to decide whether or not I am willing to put in the necessary work to get the job done." Within the first marking period of our work with performance standards, we had absolutely revolutionized the environment of our classrooms. Gone were the grumblings about how grades were something done to them. Gone were the long conferences with students about how to improve their writing without ever really helping them understand how to do so. Gone were the frustrations of trying to explain what every grading expectation looked like on every grade level. We were proving true Sizer's (1984) words: "If the goals for students are clear and relevant, student energy much more often than not will be productively focused" (p. 213).

The system of writing clear, objective standards, with the addition of checks, pluses, and minuses to indicate meeting, exceeding, or falling below standard, made a tremendous difference for us and for our students. Crystal told us, "Some teachers just stand up and tell us what the assignment is about, but the performance standards give you specific guidelines on what you have to write about." Robert added, "I like how this is done because some teachers give us a grade, but we don't know why we received the grade. When we have a check or a check plus or minus and comments in front of us, I know what I did wrong so it helps me more." Sandra, delivering a commercial-like testimonial to performance standards, voiced her satisfaction in these words: "There have been times when I have forgotten one or two of the requirements while doing the assignment, but because of my handy performance standards, I was able to catch my mistake and save many points." Finally, ever alert to signs of teacher favoritism, Roger wrote, "This prevents everyone from claiming the teacher graded some students better than others" and, perhaps more important, "It also prevents the teacher from grading some students differently." In terms of improving the atmosphere and feeling tone of a classroom, these students made powerful arguments for the standards approach.

CHAPTER 7

How Do You Keep a Good Thing Going?

MONITORING AND ADJUSTING TO KEEP UP WITH THE CLASSROOM ENVIRONMENT

Although we were beginning our third year of teaching the course together, the knots in our stomachs were as tight as ever. We were faced with new challenges that left us feeling more unsettled than we had in more than 12 months. Our class sizes were larger than ever—an average of 43 students per section—and the students' needs continued to loom larger than the content and skill areas we were planning to teach. We sensed from our roster and our initial contact with the new classes that our students were more concerned with "beating the system" than they were with the pursuit of knowledge. On anonymous surveys, students were quite candid about their lack of motivation, limited time to do homework, and general disdain for reading. They had personality, they had critical minds, they had good hearts, but did they have the desire to hold themselves to high standards? This underlying fear generated the tension in our bellies. We had been running professional development workshops explaining how empowering a standards-based curriculum could be for both teachers and students, and here we were secretly afraid that the challenges that faced us would be too much for any reform idea to overcome. Even though the goal of our district is "continuous improvement," we sympathized with other teachers' fears that we might "never arrive" (Wasley, 1994, p. 48).

These emotions introduced us to one of the dimensions of the teaching profession that is rarely discussed in education courses or literature: How do you keep a good thing going? Every school year, teachers in our district were expected to refine their teaching to include new approaches and goals as dictated by their own ideas, department initiatives, administrators' visions, and state and national directives. In addition, teachers had to prepare themselves to unlock the mystery of the dynamics of each class and the depths of their interest level and work ethic, chemistry with the teacher, and willingness to learn. On top of these annual changes, we also now were thrust into the spotlight in our school district as "pioneers" of standards-based work.

We wrestled with the new responsibilities that we believed our initial success had laid on us—that we had to prove on a daily basis that our ideas were worth the struggle to change.

MOTIVATING STUDENTS

After our initial introductions about the course and our expectations, the real work of the year began. On the second day of school, we explained the first project-based assessment students would be asked to complete—contemplating the role of myth and reality in the retelling of events. Students were asked to write a two-paragraph essay centered around a family myth. In the first paragraph, each student had to recount a family story that had been told and retold since early childhood. In the second paragraph, the student then assumed the role of the "truth-seeker" to determine how much of the story was "real" and how much had been fictionalized over the years. We explained to the students the three performance standards they were expected to meet:

- The student's assignment is a minimum of one page.
- The student recounts a long-held family story.
- The student analyzes both the myth and reality present in the story.

We then instructed students that because this task was a homework assignment, they would receive a check plus if their work had exceeded the standard, a check if they had met standard, a check minus if they had made an attempt to meet standard but needed to develop their work more in that area, or a zero if a good-faith attempt had not been made to meet the standard. We often used this system to evaluate tasks similar to this one—too small to be a significant grade but too large to be a regular homework assignment. Instead of attaching numerical grades to these tasks, students earned "credits," one for each standard. Therefore, this task was worth three homework credits. A check plus or a check resulted in full credit for the standard, a check minus and a zero resulted in no credit. Not only did this approach enable students to begin to familiarize themselves with meeting standards, but it ensured that all assignments contained certain expectations of quality work.

Once we had finished reviewing the directions and the performance standards used for evaluation of student work, we introduced the reading to be used to prepare students to be able to be successful on the task. Although we had always believed that the connections were obvious between materials we assigned and the work we asked our students to complete, we found that our students invested more effort and thoughtfulness into the materials when they believed that performance standards enabled them to complete the assessment in a more successful manner. Today was the first time they were learning this lesson for themselves as they began to read an interpretation of a Romanian legend recounted in a section of Mircea Eliade's (1954) *The Myth of the Eternal Return.* The narrator of the tale explained that he was researching an ancient legend about a jealous mountain fairy who pushed a young man off of a cliff on the eve of his wedding because she could not bear to see him marry. As the narrator researched the tragic story, he came upon a woman who claimed to be the jilted bride of "long, long ago" who recounted a much more mundane series of events (her fiancé had slipped and fallen off the cliff approximately 40 years earlier). When the narrator confronted the villagers with the "real" version of the incident, the villagers believed that the woman had lost her mind. Most profound, however, was the narrator's final remark that perhaps "it was the myth that told the truth."

After reading the excerpt from Eliade, we engaged our students in a heated debate about whether the mountain fairy existed. "Do you believe in mountain fairies?" one of us asked the class. Most of the students snickered and shook their heads, indicating the ludicrous nature of the question. "Raise your hand if you believe that it was possible that the mountain fairy existed." One and a half hands were raised in the air. (A shy student in the middle of the room kept sort of raising her hand, both out of general uncertainty about the idea and fear of going against the vehemence of 90% of her classmates.) Kim, the only other believer in the room so far, said, "I clapped my hands for Tinker Bell in *Peter Pan*, so I guess I can buy this story, too." While a few students quickly reminisced about watching *Peter Pan* when they were little kids, they remained unmoved about their position on mountain fairies. When we pressed them about whether they, too, had clapped their hands for Tinker Bell, someone exclaimed from the back of the room, "That was kid's stuff. We didn't know any better then." Once again, most of the class nodded in agreement. Thirty-five minutes later, our discussion had included an analysis of the difference in perspectives between children and adults, whether it was possible to explain an event objectively, why people embellish stories when they retell them, and what benefits are gained when the "real" story is fictionalized. As the debate began to subside, one student asked, "What does this have to do with writing about one of our family stories?" Just as one of us was about to respond, another student chimed in, "You know, talking about our own family mountain fairies. Stories that our parents have always told us that we thought were a little bizarre, but never really cared enough to try to contradict." We were beginning to establish competence in the classroom. At least one student already understood the purpose motivating the work we did in the classroom.

The next day we received a wonderfully diverse pile of responses including a story about how opals were a cursed family jewel, how lightning always resulted in bad luck, and how some spiritual power helped a student's parents to meet and fall in love. More than 60% of the class received all three credits on the task. Approximately 10% of the students did not really understand how to analyze the family legend, either because they were still wrestling with the concepts or because they did not really see the mythical elements in the story. The remaining 30%, however, received two out of three credits because their work did not meet the minimum length requirement of one page. When we pressed those students about why they had not worked harder to meet this standard, we received the typical responses.

"I didn't have time to finish. Sports practice always takes a lot out of me in the beginning of the year."

"Did not feel like writing any more."

"I ran out of stuff to say. Besides, isn't it quality, not quantity, that counts?"

As we continued to notice the trend among students to fail to meet some of the more basic standards, such as length requirement, we also continued to have an open dialogue with the whole class about the issue. "If you know that your work is expected to be a certain length or organized in a certain format in order to meet the standard, why wouldn't you just do that?" Two of the more outspoken students were quick to respond.

"I think it is unfair of you two to force us to create work in the way that you want it. Aren't we old enough by now to be able to figure out what is the best way for us to express ourselves?"

"Why do you care so much if we meet the standard or not? It's our grades, not yours. No one puts a mark on your work."

The rest of the class mainly sat there and shrugged their shoulders. Although we were only 4 weeks into the school year, it became clear that this was going to be a major issue this year: motivating students to care enough to meet the expectations laid out for them.

As the school year rolled on, students became more accustomed to the role of performance standards in the evaluation process. They reacted positively to being informed about expectations for their work when the directions were given out, and many students continued to take advantage of opportunities to revise their work to meet or exceed certain standards with which they had originally struggled. While some students continued to lose the battle to motivate themselves to attempt to meet all the standards, the classes as a whole believed that the standards were realistic, attainable, and worthwhile.

GUIDING A MAJOR CLASS PROJECT

The mood began to change, however, when we introduced the research paper. The research-paper component was an English department requirement for all eleventh-grade students in the high school. Because this was an American Studies curriculum, we broadened the scope of the task to include not only a discussion of an American novel but also how it related to a specific social or political reform movement during the time it was published. The essential question for that marking period was: "What is reform?" Every minute of class discussion, as well as every piece of writing and reading, focused on that question, yet we knew immediately that we had a problem. To analyze both a historical time period and a piece of literature, and to discuss the interaction between the two, would be a hopeless task for many of our students. Although we had been working with them on honing their reading comprehension skills, the diversity of reading abilities made it difficult to work at a level that was comfortable yet challenging for each student. Some of our students struggled to retain more than five pages of reading per night. Other students had to work with tutors during a structured study time during the school day or with their parents at night in order to process a short story or a chapter from a novel. Even among those students who had stronger reading comprehension skills, many failed to find the time to complete the assignment and found themselves rushing through the sections at 2:00 A.M. or in the hallway before class began. The thought of reading an entire novel seemed a daunting task. Although we had read *The Great Gatsby* together several weeks earlier, many of the students dreaded those 2 weeks because they "had no clue" about what was going on. In fact, when we asked the class if they were shocked by how many people were killed in the last chapter, many of them looked at us as if we were crazy.

"Somebody died? Who?"

"You mean, finally something good happens and we missed it?"

"Why can't this guy write what happens clearer so we actually can follow what's going on?"

"This really can't be that famous a novel. Who can even follow it?"

Introducing the Task

This recent experience coupled with a genuine dislike for reading created a high anxiety level when we told students that they were expected to independently read a novel from the list we provided for them. The research paper was a task of great complexity in an interdisciplinary course, requiring students to read a novel critically and thoughtfully, to research its literary acceptance, and to link it to a corresponding political or social reform. In the same 10-week period, we needed to teach them about the various reform movements and help them clarify their own answer to the essential question "What is reform?" both for ordinary classwork and for the research paper.

Despite our understanding of the importance of preparing students to read by engaging in pre-discussions and devoting significant time to asking questions to drive students deeper into the reading, we tried to incorporate more response to literature without sacrificing additional time. This formula is generally the death of much of school reform. We tell participants in our workshops that it is impossible to shift to a standards-based curriculum and teach everything included in their curriculum right now. To get there, we had to accept the old adage "less is more" (Sizer, 1986, p. 40). Our chances to help students learn would improve dramatically, we felt, if we could cover less in greater depth rather than more superficially. Also, when we had combined two disciplines into one course, we had soon realized that we could never cover everything. Our job was to create a big picture for our course that would make sense to us and to students. Our research-paper assignment sacrificed the time necessary to discuss literature as literature.

From the beginning, we tried to make the task as manageable as possible: assisting students in finding a novel with which they felt comfortable (in terms of both subject matter and reading level), giving them additional class time to get acclimated to the characters and to troubleshoot any questions, and requiring a reader-response journal that would help make them more accountable and, we hoped, more sensitive readers. To complete the journal, students were expected to record two to three significant quotations per chapter and then explain that significance in their own words. We explained that completing the journal would not only earn them points toward their overall research-paper grade (alleviating some of the pressure of the final draft) but would also give them a wealth of information to use when it came time to write an analysis of their individual novels. Despite constant monitoring of their progress and offers to provide additional assistance, when the journals were due, the majority of the class made it clear that they were unhappy about our requirement.

"Why can't we just read a book without having to think about it?"

"Do you really expect us to be able to finish this novel and understand it if we don't talk about it as a class?"

"I can just write down a bunch of quotes and do well on the assignment without even having to read the book? What a waste of time."

Although we were accustomed to hearing complaints immediately before a major assignment was due, we were disturbed by the students' pervasive lack of desire and initiative. We sincerely believed that reading the novels would help students understand what reform meant in a given period and would enhance their insight into the essential question. We also believed that the standards had clearly explained the expectations and that we also had informed them about the value of the task in helping them to understand the novel and improving their overall performance on the research paper. When we sat down with the class to discuss our mutual concerns, they made it clear that they understood exactly what we were asking them to do and why we were asking them to do it—but many of them still did not believe that it was important, and there was little we could say to change their minds.

The Central Phases of the Work

Once they had read the novel and completed the journal, they next had to complete three phases of writing: a four- to five-page analysis of the novel, a four- to five-page overview of the related social or political reform movement, and a two-page review of how literary critics had received the novel when it was first published. Each piece was to be read and graded separately with its own set of performance standards, and we built in time to discuss work and troubleshoot each section. We gave them approximately 6 weeks to complete a minimum of 10 pages of writing. Our students really had grown as writers by this point in the year. The previous marking period had been a writing-intensive one in which students wrote two- to three-page essays at least every other week. They had become very familiar with the performance standards required in every writing assignment:

- The student provides an overview of his or her ideas in the introduction through the thesis statement and breakdown of topics.
- The student develops one topic in each body paragraph.
- The student creates transitions to indicate how the topics relate to one another and to the thesis statement.
- The student proofreads his or her work to eliminate mechanical errors (grammar, punctuation, spelling, etc.).

These standards also were included in the research paper writing, in addition to the standards specific to each component of the research project. While the students felt comfortable that they could achieve these standards on smaller writing assignments, they were more insecure about their ability to pull together this larger task. When we gave them time to work independently on research and writing, many of them just sat there, not sure of how or where to begin. When we prodded them to find out what was holding them back, many just looked at us in defeat: "I just have no idea how to get started." For the most part, we were dealing with students of goodwill who tried to meet our expectations, and they had tried to discipline themselves to be self-directed researchers, readers, and writers. But, during the later weeks of the marking period, several parents called us voicing concern about the high stress level and late nights caused by the assignment. One parent went as far as to claim that the paper "is ruining the quality of family life because my child is so concerned about it all of the time."

Reflecting on the Experience

The anxiety level experienced by all parties—parents, students, and teachers—taught all of us an important lesson about the use of standards in the classroom. The standards we had established for the research paper felt out of reach to our students and their parents. Even though the task was an English department requirement, even though students would be expected to produce similar work in college, even though we had broken the assignment down into manageable steps, and even though students had an ample amount of time to complete it, we remained unable to defuse the tension. It was not until the end of the school year that students could see the benefits of having gone through the experience. In the reflection segment of the portfolio (we call it the "Note From the Author"), many students discussed their change of heart about the assignment.

"I can't believe I got through it. But now that I did, I am amazed at what I wrote. I am sure that this will help me handle the next research paper I have to do better."

"It was neat to look back and see how much I learned about the history and the novel. I was surprised by some of the ideas I came up with."

"I wish that I was able to follow through better. Even though I worked hard, I could have done much better if I had worked more consistently."

"I really felt a sense of accomplishment when I saw how all of the pieces came together. I can't believe I actually wrote 12 pages!"

While we were pleased to read that the majority of our students now agreed about the value of the research paper, the question of whether or not the assignment needed substantial revision loomed large for us. Clearly, our students did not feel competent throughout the duration of the assignment. Were our standards too high here for the population we were teaching? Did we damage the positive learning environment in our classroom by asking students (and parents) to stretch beyond what seemed possible? Had our essential question been too weak to draw students deeper into the assignment? At the heart of a standards-based curriculum lies a professional estimation of what students know and should be able to do. Once we made this estimation based on the level of the students we were teaching and the content area we were responsible for, we crafted those convictions into thoughtful essential questions, created cogent content and performance standards and assessments, and communicated those to our students so that they could become more successful workers and learners. We were never so naive as to expect that our students would embrace the opportunity to write a research paper, but we did expect that they would do so more successfully because of the standards.

Creating a competent classroom does not mean that students will always appreciate the significance of the work they produce. The goal remains, however, to have students gain a deeper appreciation of this on a more regular basis. We have the teaching experience and the professional development to know that the standards did help the students that year to craft a better overall product and that it was a worthwhile activity. The educational dilemma of sticking with our professional estimations in the face of serious criticism will never be easy to handle, no matter how much we refine our work. We believe that if teachers continuously make the effort to articulate to their students through their essential questions why the work they are doing is meaningful and how standards will assist their pursuit of success, then students will not only believe in their competence but will also take the necessary actions to demonstrate it. We agree with Theodore Sizer's (1984) succinct appraisal that "a successful class is one in which student and teachers agree on what they are about and the rules of the academic game" (p. 154). In addition, if we wanted students to produce quality work, they had to perceive it as worthwhile. "Adolescents as well as adults learn only what they want to learn, what they are convinced is important, what inspires them" (Sizer, 1992, p. 143). These quotes illustrate clearly how the interrelationship of essential questions and standards improves the competence of a classroom.

This message becomes ever more important to us as more and more teachers can be heard in our building muttering about how "kids are not what they used to be" and bemoaning the lack of the work ethic they see in their classrooms. Although we, too, believed that our students could have invested more in their work that year, we were also astounded by the minimal amount of time left in their day for homework after school and their other activities. One day when there were about 5 minutes left before the bell rang, we fell into a casual conversation with a group of students complaining about their schedules for the rest of the day. More than 50% of our students worked a minimum of 10 hours per week. Many of them also competed in sports programs, participated in extracurricular activities, received or gave tutoring, and contributed volunteer hours to service projects. In their spare time, they babysat for their younger siblings or the neighbors' kids, did chores for their parents, went to the mall, talked on the phone, and hung out with their friends. We were shocked to hear that almost none of the students started their homework before 10:00 p.m. They seemed to be suffering from the same dilemma in their daily lives that we had struggled with in the early phases of our curriculum work: trying to accomplish too many tasks without a clear understanding of what was most important.

BRINGING STUDENTS TO SELF-ASSESSMENT

A later component we added to our standards work was self-assessment. Although we had always encouraged students to do this when surveying or proofreading their own work, we never formally included it as a class requirement. We had been reluctant to require self-assessment primarily for two reasons. First, for students to complete a thorough self-assessment in writing, we needed to allocate approximately 10 minutes of class time. While that may seem relatively trivial, considering that students completed approximately eight to ten tasks per marking period, that is more than two full class periods "lost" to the activity per quarter. Second, both we and our students were uncertain of the value of the activity. When we had tried to have students self-assess, they had done so in a relatively superficial manner, reluctantly discussing such fundamental issues as the organization of their ideas, the depth of their discussion, and their understanding of key materials. As we discussed in Chapter 6, we had experimented with self-evaluation with student oral presentations in the fall of our first year with standards, and it had helped individual students, but we had not tried anything systematic. Because many of the students did not invest themselves in their comments, we did not invest much in reading their responses. The result was that we had lapsed back into the traditional paradigm in which students produce the work and teachers produce the grades.

The next spring, however, when we were teaching a professional development workshop, an English teacher questioned us about whether we found that our students developed an improved capacity for self-assessment when we used performance standards. We cautiously responded: "We do not have a lot to say on the subject. The opportunity is there for self-assessment, but we have not focused on it yet in our classes." While the teacher who posed the question seemed satisfied with our noncommittal response, we felt oddly guilty. Self-assessment was always something that we "wished" we had the time to do, but we believed that the curricular demands just did not afford us that "luxury." In addition, it was one of the six goals of quality school work articulated by William Glasser (1992). As we mulled over the issue during that summer, we decided that we needed to make this more of a priority for the following school year.

In order to try to make this a more meaningful experience for all parties, we eased into the process that fall. Initially, we asked students just to "guess" what they thought their grade would be on each standard (marking a check plus, check, check minus, or zero). Although the students thought they were grading themselves a little haphazardly in the beginning, their marks actually were quite close to our own. As the next step, we had students act as shadow graders—they would grade other students during the delivery of oral or visual presentations alongside one of us. We would discuss the mark we thought the student performer earned on each standard, and then, based on the discussion, the student grader would write a comment on the grade sheet. This step was quite successful. Many students commented to us that the experience gave them a clearer understanding of how to meet and exceed standard in their own work. The more serious mental obstacle was to ease student concerns about being graded by their peers. Many still believed that grading was an artform that could be fairly executed only by a professional. Our students definitely took a while to warm up to the idea. One student offhandedly commented to another, "They're just doing this so they don't have to do any work." Another student complained about the shadow grader evaluating her performance: "I really would feel more comfortable if you did it instead. I worked too hard to have him grade me." Although we appreciated the amount of faith the students had in us, we also wanted them to realize that any member of the class who had a solid understanding both of the task and of the standards could come up with a reasonable evaluation of the final product.

By the third marking period of the second year, we felt that students were beginning to trust their ability to both understand and navigate the standards. We then incorporated a new performance standard on each evaluation sheet:

- The student accurately self-assesses his or her work.

Our goal was to empower students to become accurate evaluators of their own work. If we could achieve this goal, we could finally achieve part of the original vision that had prompted us to begin this journey—defusing our students' frustration with the grading process. They ultimately would become accountable to themselves. Our role would also shift from "judge and jury" to one of a "critical friend" and "recordkeeper." In order to make this transition, however, students needed to be trained to use the performance standards properly. By adding the additional standard that valued "accuracy," students would learn through practice how their work measured up to the standard. Students earned a check plus for this new standard if their self-evaluation of their work was identical to our own, a check if the scores were different on one or two performance standards, a check minus if there were three or four differences, or a zero if the student scored himself or herself differently on more than four standards. Because we also valued the thought behind the evaluation, the student would receive a zero if he or she did not write comments indicating why a check plus or check minus was given. We informed the students that they had received enough practice with self-assessment to evaluate their own work fairly and that we would expect them to self-assess their work for the entire last semester. We explained that this exercise would also make them more successful because it would make them accountable to themselves for their grade. This step would provide the final shift to make grading not something that was "done to them" by their teachers, but rather the expectations they had for their own performance. By mid-February of the school year, our students definitely had the self-assessment system down. The day an assignment was due, the students would come into the room, automatically pick up a clean copy of the standards, sit in their seats, and evaluate their work. Regardless of their experience with the procedure, students still spent about 10 minutes to complete the evaluation. Many students also continued to agonize over the process. It was typical to see students bent over their papers with furrowed brows, silently debating between two marks on a standard. We encouraged students who were stuck on a standard to ask a neighbor for advice or to ask one of us a clarifying question. Once we received the evaluation sheets from the students, we tailored our grading role so that we reacted not only to their work but also to their own comments. Not only were we pleasantly surprised by the accuracy and insight of their evaluations, but we also were excited to have the time and the opportunity to make more personalized remarks on each paper. Take one of the standards referred to earlier for a writing assignment:

- The student creates transitions to indicate how the topics relate to one another and to the thesis statement.

One student gave his paper a check minus on this standard based on his belief that "the topics are obvious in each paragraph, but I guess I never come right out and explain the connections. I'm not really sure how to do that." Next to his comment on the grading sheet, we replied, "You are right about needing to explain the connections. Generally, the easiest place to make the transitions is in the first sentence of the new paragraph. Try inserting a new phrase or sentence at the beginning of each body paragraph." Then we illustrated with a sample transition statement relevant to his work.

Self-assessment became a win–win situation for everyone: The students took responsibility for the major criticism and success of their work, we had the time to write more specific advice because the students included the more basic comments, and the students became much more adept at self-reflection, making them more independent workers.

After 3 years developing and refining this revolution, we were intoxicated by the power, positive energy, and skill development possible in a competent classroom. We were also fully cognizant of the considerable amount of time, practice, multiple explanations, and patience it took us to establish and foster such a learning environment. As we, along with our students, began to savor the feeling of competence, a new question began to emerge: Why aren't more teachers using this approach? The short answer was that this was an area that we "developed" based on "our students" and what we "perceived" to be necessary and valuable. The longer answer was that we became involved in demonstrating the wider applicability of the concepts to our peers in a meaningful and effective manner.

CHAPTER 8

How Can the Competent Classroom Work Better?

REFINING THE CONCEPT OF THE COMPETENT CLASSROOM

As we looked back over our journey to create a competent classroom, and as we reviewed our workshops and presentations to colleagues, we found that we had learned so much—not only about curricular revision but also about how to ensure that such revision proceeds more smoothly and produces more lasting effects. We cannot emphasize enough that a key ingredient for success was bringing students and parents on board with us from the very beginning. We also learned how much more can be accomplished with curricular reform when teachers are treated professionally. We found, sometimes with frustration, that true curricular revision is very gradual, not a wholesale overnight overhaul; that teachers can enter the process at whatever point feels most comfortable for them; and that this framework can inform not only an individual classroom but also an entire district. Finally, we are convinced that these concepts work only when they are applied together consistently. A competent classroom evolves through steady and consistent use of essential questions, content standards, assessments, and performance standards. Revisiting some of our experiences chronicled in the previous chapters provides the evidence to support our convictions.

BRINGING STUDENTS AND PARENTS ON BOARD

From the beginning, we recognized that communication with students and parents was the key to our success. Our original plan had been to create a new scoring system for students that would empower them in our course and increase their sense of competence. The point of all our efforts had been to demystify their learning and show them that if they knew what was expected of them in advance, they could succeed. Of course, we had to learn ourselves that what was crystal-clear to us as we wrote it might not have the same clarity for a class of high school juniors at 7:30 A.M. Students were quick to say, "But that's not what you said," when we wrote a poor, vague performance standard. We needed to be patient, to rewrite and revise our standards continually, and to recognize that their feedback was a healthy part of the growth of student ownership of the course. We also needed to practice being consistent and firm that once standards were in place they were to be followed. One of the most gratifying aspects of working with this framework was the occasions when students would come to one of us and say, "I know that I didn't follow this standard. I just paid no attention to it. May I revise?" If we fulfilled our bargain to publish essential questions, and to provide assessments and performance standards well in advance, they would understand that we were all on the same side and that the course was designed to help them demonstrate what they had learned. We have said that we looked on our relationship with our students as a contract. In such circumstances, both sides have a vested interest in the success of everyone involved.

In the same way, and for many of the same reasons, parents became our staunchest allies. We were determined that they should receive all necessary information about the course and that they should feel confident to call us with questions or concerns. We published our syllabus, described our assignments, encouraged their calls and comments, and made ourselves available beyond usual conference times. Parents want to be strong advocates for their children, and they, too, want to feel that they know what their children are studying and how their children can best succeed while at the same time being challenged academically. Parents of students who were usually successful loved the way their children's confidence could be even further reinforced and their interest sustained; parents of students who were normally less successful cheered the use of a framework that was concrete and specific enough to help their children organize themselves and maintain high academic standards. Both sets of parents applauded the fact that students could manage an academically rigorous class if the curriculum was in alignment and if students, parents, and teachers maintained a high level of communication. One of our students told us before the November conferences one year, "My parents aren't coming to see you because they say you have told them everything they need to know. None of my other teachers do that." It was the aligned curriculum that allowed us to communicate with students and parents so confidently, because we knew what we were about. Moreover, the more parents heard about what was going on in the course, the more interested and supportive they became. From essential questions to standards, the framework captured their interest and enthusiasm, too, so much so that they often expressed the wish to take American Studies themselves.

TREATING TEACHERS AS PROFESSIONALS

As we began to present workshops about curricular revision to our colleagues, we learned how important it is that teachers be treated professionally if reform is to take root. When we began to think about restructuring our course, we knew that the school year—with its sometimes unmanageable load of preparation, grading, and meetings—was the wrong time to begin. Summer is the time that teachers can call their own, the appropriate time to rethink and to plan. We were fortunate that we had the firm support of Assistant Superintendent Kuklis, who extended money for our hours of curriculum writing and provided constant encouragement along the way. When we decided to try to share our epiphanies with our colleagues, both central administration and our building principal also helped us immensely. We received a mini-grant to present three workshops but spent most of it on a luncheon for the participants, catered by the school culinary program. In addition, each teacher received release time from afternoon classes, with the principal scurrying to provide coverage. Both administrators also attended our workshop, extending yet one more vote of confidence. One teacher, renowned for her usual frazzled air, sighed and commented, "I have never been treated this professionally in 28 years." We really believed that the concepts we presented could make sense to teachers, but the combination of payment for work done, release time, and attention to comfort predisposed them to reflection and willingness to experiment.

THE PROCESS OF REVISING CURRICULUM

In most school districts, curriculum revision takes place on a schedule determined by central administration policy. Our district provided for curriculum revision in each department every 5 years, on a staggered schedule so that all departments would not be going through the process at once. These schedules ensure that change does take place, at least in a formal way. More often than not, the majority of teachers need the regularity of the schedule of revision to spur them to look at individual courses and rework them.

We began our course revision within the curricular framework supported by our assistant superintendent, but we were among the first teachers in our district to adopt it as the organizing principle of our entire curriculum. When we offered to present what we had done to our peers, fully half of the high school teachers took one of our three workshops. All expressed interest in the concepts, and many began to experiment with them. But still there was a segment of the faculty that expressed no interest in finding out about our curricular framework. They had seen many reforms come and go, and expected to see this one go as well. It was only when our administrators made essential questions and standards a district issue that every teacher received some in-service training. Even now, fully 3 years after we began, most teachers have only a rudimentary understanding of how these concepts work and are reluctant practitioners. It takes time to become proficient and courage to change everything that you have been doing without understanding fully how it can help.

THE IMPORTANCE OF MAINTAINING CURRICULAR ALIGNMENT

Despite the national movement to standards, and our feelings of pride and success based on our work with curricular alignment, we have learned that teachers need to be comfortable with the process and that they should begin to work on alignment from the point that works best for them. When we first began to revise and rewrite curriculum, we dutifully created essential questions to focus each marking period, recognizing intellectually that they were significant for maintaining both purpose and direction. However, we then thought that the standards were the recipe for success. It was by trial and error that we came to understand the importance of essential questions, and if we had to choose, that is where we would begin if we were doing it over. But after talking with teachers at various workshops over the past 2 years, we are convinced that no two teachers approach the concepts of curricular revision in the same way. For some, the essential question does not quite make sense in the context of their course. Many teachers of subjects such as mathematics and languages feel that their subject matter has such strong intrinsic organization that essential questions are superfluous and basically gimmicky. Some teachers believe that the course should be structured and planned backward from an "authentic" assessment, and that that is the correct place to begin. Others insist that the content standards represent what they teach, and would start from them. Indeed, many teachers have already worked in systems where they were given their content standards and performance standards in advance. They need to enter the process there, to adapt what they have to do to the needs of their students.

Teachers who would like to try these concepts to create an aligned curriculum can experiment from whichever point in the process they are most familiar and comfortable with. If they are like us, they will eventually come to the realization that each component succeeds because of the alignment of the whole. No matter the order in which essential questions, content standards, assessments, and performance standards are created, the whole is greater than the sum of the parts and gives every aspect of the curriculum unity and purpose every day.

PREPARING STUDENTS FOR STATE ASSESSMENTS

As teachers revisit curricula, lesson plans, and assessments to determine how to integrate essential questions and standards, they must also address the reality of high-stakes testing in their school district. National tests that measure student aptitude and affect college admission have significantly influenced the way teachers teach specific skill areas such as reading, writing, and problem solving. The role and significance of state content-based examinations are not as established in the school culture. Over the past 5 to 10 years, an increasing number of states have created and mandated assessments to provide a more comprehensive report of scholastic achievement in the region. Although student performance on these assessments may have little impact on their students' present or future academic plans, they have a significant impact on the public image of the individual school district. Annual state reports indicate the school's overall performance as well as comparing its performance with that of other schools in the surrounding area.

Teachers want their students to perform well on these assessments, but they raise legitimate concerns about how to prepare students for the test and teach the required curriculum simultaneously. While most states have created content standards for each area of their assessments, these standards tend to be cumbersome for teachers to work with because of their length and lack of clarity. During our workshops with teachers, we are often asked how to address these challenges in a way that is best for students. The best piece of advice we can give to teachers is to make the assessment a partner rather than an enemy. If the students know that the teacher resents the intrusion of the assessment into the "real work" that would otherwise be done, students will resent the experience as well. We encourage teachers to identify content standards that drive the assessment and work to incorporate those standards into their curriculum.

Because high-stakes tests can threaten the feeling of competence in the classroom, teachers must take ownership of the testing experience. They are responsible for presenting the content standards, practice materials, and instructional strategies to their students. Teachers can clarify language, create their own practice experiences based on concepts and materials in their curriculum, and reinforce the value of the essential skills that are being tested (without mentioning the test at all). All these strategies ensure that the learning environment continues to be a positive partnership of teachers and students. While this approach is more laborious than "teaching to the test," it enables teachers to incorporate the valuable skills and strategies in the state assessment without sacrificing the curricular alignment necessary to maintain a competent classroom.

CONTINUING THE JOURNEY

It is easy to become discouraged when the first attempts at any reform meet with hostility or apathy. Students can resist any attempt to make them feel accountable and to close their loopholes. Standards can be poorly written and cause the teacher headaches. Prize assessments can become suddenly useless when they no longer fit into an aligned curriculum. Essential questions may prove more limited on a trial than they seemed. For all these reasons, teachers become frustrated and may abandon the ideas or drop them until they can reflect on how to make them work. Our experience has been that the only way to make curricular alignment work is to practice it each and every day. We have had many setbacks, but we have met with gradual success as we kept trying. We recommend that teachers experiment gradually and introduce the concepts slowly, so that they can maintain their consistency. Introducing everything at once is overwhelming, for both students and teachers.

Working to create a competent classroom has been the professional experience of a lifetime, one worth all the time and effort it cost. We have been privileged to see how much can be done to improve curriculum when teachers are treated as professionals, when the district becomes involved actively and supportively in reform, and when professionals get a chance to share ideas and experiences. It has been exciting to try to forge a community of students, teachers, and parents who communicate effectively to support student learning, and a classroom where students have a better chance to succeed because they know what is expected of them. It has been said that all journeys begin with a single step. Each step of our journey has brought us closer to achieving a competent classroom. We wish others the same good fortune on their professional journey.

American Studies Curriculum

We developed the first curriculum in the summer of 1997 and continued to improve upon it over the next 2 years. We wrote the second American Studies curriculum in conjunction with two other colleagues, Charles Mann and Jeanetta Miller. It was adopted by the board of education in August 1999. The impetus for this new version was to achieve a more equitable balance between literature and history throughout the curriculum and to have a unified approach for both honors and college preparatory students. Both curricula reflect the values and concepts delineated throughout the text.

OUR ORIGINAL AMERICAN STUDIES CURRICULUM—*SUMMER 1997*

Marking Period 1: Immigration and the American Dream

CURRICULUM COMPONENT	CONTENT FOCUS: IMMIGRATION AND THE AMERICAN DREAM	SKILL FOCUS: PRESENTATION SKILLS
Essential question	Who is entitled to the American Dream?	How does working with others enhance the quality of thought?
Content standard	The student will be able to assess the impact of immigration on American society.	The student will be able to work effectively with other students to produce a persuasive presentation.
Instructional objectives	1. The student will determine the factors that prompted each wave of immigration. 2. The student will analyze the economic role of immigrants in the building of the American empire. 3. The student will discuss the diversity of social issues raised when different cultures were introduced into American society. 4. The student will read accounts of immigrant life and distinguish between their myths and their reality. 5. The student will draw connections between American literature and historical waves of immigration.	1. The student will use narration and expository writing, speaking, and presentation skills. 2. The student will build on reading comprehension skills by working with a variety of primary source documents, both historical and literary. 3. The student will practice team-building skills by completing a variety of small-group tasks.
Performance assessment	The student will conduct a paired writing debate to a congressional representative, explaining his or her opinion on the topic: Who should be entitled to the American Dream?	Same as for Content Focus.
Performance standards	1. The student identifies the factors that prompted each wave of immigration. 2. The student evaluates the economic role of immigrants in the building of the American empire. 3. The student analyzes social issues raised due to the influx of immigrants.	1. The student will create an organizational framework to discuss each main point—a thesis, one topic per body paragraph, and topic sentences. 2. The student will use information from packet material and class discussions to support his or her ideas. 3. The student will address the questions and comments raised by his or her paired writing partner.

MARKING PERIOD 2: WORK AND PLAY

CURRICULUM COMPONENT	CONTENT FOCUS: WORK AND PLAY	SKILL FOCUS: THE WRITING PROCESS
Essential question	What do work and play say about the quality of American life?	How does the use of reading and writing strategies enhance the quality of thought?
Content standard	The student will be able to articulate how predominant forms of work and play shaped the American Dream.	The student will improve his or her ability to articulate ideas in writing.
Instructional objectives	1. The student will examine the predominant forms of work and play in each time period. 2. The student will trace the evolution of the American Dream in each time period. 3. The student will draw connections between American literature and work, play, and the American Dream.	1. The student will use the techniques of narration, description, exposition, and persuasion in writing. 2. The student will build on reading comprehension skills by working with a variety of primary source documents, both historical and literary. 3. The student will practice effective strategies to enhance reading comprehension. 4. The student will study vocabulary to enhance his or her ability to read and communicate.
Performance assessment	The student will compose a visual essay that delineates the major trends in work and play in America and how those trends impacted the American Dream.	Same as for Content Focus.
Performance standards	1. The student will provide images for work, play, and the American Dream. 2. The student will create captions on each page to explain the context and relevance of the image(s). 3. The student will evaluate the evolution of work, play, and the American Dream throughout U.S. history.	1. The student will organize the visual essay according to the requirements of the assignment. 2. The student will provide detail to elucidate the context and significance of each image. 3. The student will reflect on the images used for work, play, and the American Dream to draw connections between time periods.

MARKING PERIOD 3: POLITICAL MOVEMENTS AND SOCIAL REFORM

CURRICULUM COMPONENT	CONTENT FOCUS: POLITICAL MOVEMENTS AND SOCIAL REFORM	SKILL FOCUS: PERSUASIVE PRESENTATIONS
Essential question	What is reform?	What techniques of persuasion are most effective in creating and sustaining change?
Content standard	The student will be able to explore one social or political movement in detail through the establishment of connections between American history and literature.	The student will be able to employ techniques of persuasion in a variety of written and public-speaking tasks.
Instructional objectives	1. The student will study the forces required to ignite meaningful political and/or social change. 2. The student will examine the role of activists and political leaders in effecting change in American society. 3. The student will assess the overall impact of the reform movement and how it affected the lives of those it was intended to help.	1. The student will practice persuasive writing, speaking, and presentation skills. 2. The student will build on reading comprehension skills by working with a variety of primary source documents, both historical and literary. 3. The student will complete the process of writing a research paper. 4. The student will use team-building skills to complete a variety of group tasks.
Performance assessment	The student will define the meaning of reform based on his or her study of one political movement or social reform in the research paper.	The student will write a research paper that draws on and explains the connections between an American political movement or social reform and a relevant work of American literature.
Performance standards	1. The student will demonstrate an understanding of the full time range of the political movement or social reform. 2. The student will articulate a definition for reform and what elements are required to create permanent change. 3. The student will evaluate the success of the reform movement he or she studied in the research paper. 4. The student will use information from primary and secondary sources and the novel read in conjunction with the reform movement.	1. The student will provide transitions between each piece to connect major ideas. 2. The student will revise the research paper based on the comments made on rough drafts. 3. The student will use quotations effectively by explaining their context and relevance to the thesis. 4. The student will create an organizational framework for the paper.

MARKING PERIOD 4: AMERICAN WARS

CURRICULUM COMPONENT	CONTENT FOCUS: AMERICAN WARS	SKILL FOCUS: ART OF EXPRESSION
Essential question	How has war shaped the image of America?	How do artistic and visual expressions of war shape our understanding?
Content standard	The student will be able to assess the impact of war on the United States.	The student will be able to use writing to capture the emotions and imagery evoked by visual and artistic expressions of war.
Instructional objectives	1. The student will study the various causes that brought America into war. 2. The student will evaluate the factual and emotional content of propaganda on the home front. 3. The student will trace American foreign policy by analyzing common themes and drawing connections. 4. The student will identify gains and losses as a result of war. 5. The student will read, analyze, and evaluate literature of each period to draw connections between war on the historic large scale and the personal microcosm.	1. The student will respond to questions on theme and characters based on viewing films of the period. 2. The student will extract major points from oral presentations and will record them in a meaningful and accessible manner. 3. The student will study photographs and other visual representations of war to gain further insights into the impact of war. 4. The student will create poetry that demonstrates an appreciation of the emotional impact of war, while maintaining historical accuracy.
Performance assessment	Based on one of the wars studied during the marking period, students will deliver an oral presentation that answers the essential question. The presentation will include: recitation of a poem, discussion of a relevant piece of literature, review of causes that brought America into war, assessment of how the war tied into American foreign policy, and analysis of major gains and losses as a result of the war.	Same as for Content Focus.
Performance standards	1. The student will assess the impact of the war on the American psyche and on American foreign policy. 2. The student's poem will provide insight about the war's impact 3. The student will explain how a relevant piece of literature reveals the war's impact.	1. The student will present a dramatic reading of a poem. 2. The student will establish a connection with the audience through tone, volume, energy level, and eye contact. 3. The student will create an overview of the content of the presentation.

REVISED AMERICAN STUDIES CURRICULUM—*SUMMER 1999*

MARKING PERIOD 1: THE CITY ON THE HILL

CURRICULUM COMPONENT	CONTENT FOCUS
Essential question	What does it mean to be an American?
Content standard	The student will be able to assess the development of nationhood and the emergence of an American aesthetic.
Instructional objectives	The student identifies the motives that prompted people to colonize the New World.
	The student assesses how expectations of the New World shaped the political, social, and economic structure.
	The student examines the common values that created the American identity.
	The student analyzes how the struggle for freedom impacted American expression.
Performance assessment	The student chronicles three to four key events/concepts that demonstrate the development of nationhood and the emergence of an American aesthetic. Based on this work, the student concludes what it meant to be an American in 1876. The student then speculates about the contemporary relevance of this definition.
Performance standards	The student demonstrates that the three to four events selected are key developments in the emergence of nationhood and the American aesthetic.
	The student uses a variety of historical and literary sources to complete the task.
	The student develops a definition of what it meant to be an American in 1876.
	The student compares the values that shaped the American identity between 1876 and the present.

MARKING PERIOD 2: UNCLE SAM NEEDS YOU

CURRICULUM COMPONENT	CONTENT FOCUS
Essential question	Would you die for your country?
Content standard	The student will be able to evaluate how our response to foreign threats impacts individual lives and American culture.
Instructional objectives	The student examines what factors/principles prompt America to use force.
	The student evaluates how American society responds to perceived threats.
	The student analyzes how patriotism determines form and content of public expression during times of crisis.
	The student explores how dissenting forms of expression attempt to challenge public opinion.
	The student assesses the lessons the public has learned through both our evolving understanding of the crisis and how that crisis is portrayed.
Performance assessment	The student delivers an oral presentation articulating what criteria he or she believes should be met in order to participate in a military conflict. This discussion incorporates foreign policy principles, patriotic and dissenting forms of expression, and major outcomes of the crisis.
Performance standards	The student develops a minimum of four criteria necessary for participation in a military conflict.
	The student highlights examples from a minimum of three conflicts studied over the course of the marking period to justify the criteria.
	The student incorporates a variety of forms of expression to represent the range in public opinion.

MARKING PERIOD 3: "WE THE PEOPLE"

CURRICULUM COMPONENT	CONTENT FOCUS
Essential question	Who are "we the people"?
Content standard	The student will be able to discuss the tension between the existence of disenfranchisement and democratic ideals.
Instructional objectives	The student defines the term *disenfranchisement* and examines how it applies to a variety of groups, including African Americans, women, and immigrants. The student studies the forces required to ignite meaningful political, social, or economic change. The student examines the role of activists and authors in effecting change in American society. The student analyzes the persuasive strategies employed by reformers in their efforts to garner support.
Performance assessment	By exploring the various disenfranchised groups studied this marking period, the student focuses on the attitudes, ideas, and actions that inspired change in the definition of "we the people." The student also examines the impact of these successes and failures on contemporary life.
Performance standards	The student defines the term *disenfranchisement.* The student examines the reform efforts to include disenfranchised groups in mainstream American society. The student uses a variety of sources to demonstrate the political, social, economic, and aesthetic impact of disenfranchisement on American society. The student answers the essential question, Who are "we the people" in reference to contemporary times?

Marking Period 4: Sustaining the City on the Hill

Curriculum Component	Content Focus
Essential question	Are we in it for the money?
Content standard	The student will be able to examine the degree to which materialism colors individual and collective action.
Instructional objectives	The student analyzes the impact of the Industrial Revolution on American life.
	The student examines the evolving importance of the consumer in American culture.
	The student evaluates the tension between materialistic ambitions and social conscience.
	The student explores the aesthetic response to dramatic economic changes.
	The student evaluates how forms of expression shape public opinion.
Performance assessment	The student completes an analysis of individual and collective action based on completion of four tasks: a resume, an analysis of that resume, a volunteer service project, and a reflection.
Performance standards	The student creates a resume that documents his or her employment and volunteer experience.
	The student analyzes the factors that prompted his or her participation in employment vs. volunteer experience.
	The student plans and executes a volunteer service project.
	The student reflects on the personal impact of the project and its link to the essential question: "Are we in it for the money?"
	The student establishes a connection between his or her mindset about money with the cultural discussion on American materialism.

Performance Standards

Creating Performance Standards

A performance standard is a statement that articulates your expectation about what standard all students are expected to meet for a given criterion. In other words, it describes what a good assignment looks like.

> *Example:* Value = Using a variety of sources to support your own ideas.
> Standard = The student uses a minimum of three sources to support his or her ideas.

The standard describes an action of the student or a quality of his or her final product.

> *Example:* Student-based = The student uses . . .
> The student explains . . .
> The student describes . . .
> Product-based = The student's poem . . .
> The student's visual depiction . . .
> The student's essay . . .

The language of the performance standard should be as clear and objective as possible.

> *Example:* Subjective standard = The student's writing is flowing and easy to follow.
> Less subjective standard = The student's writing is easy to follow because of his or her use of transitions and topic sentences.

The performance standard addresses one key value or criterion.

> *Example:* One value/criterion = The student organizes his or her ideas into a five-paragraph essay.
> Many values/criteria = The student creates a clear organizational structure by creating a five-paragraph essay, writing transition statements, and crafting clear topic sentences.

NOTE: Although you can create a standard with more than one value/criterion, it becomes more difficult to evaluate students on a specific standard because they may meet your expectations for some of the values/criteria but fall below standard for other values/criteria.

Suggested Verbs to Use When Writing Performance Standards

When writing student-based performance standards, the following verbs may be useful to help you articulate your expectations for each value or criterion:

allocates	monitors
applies	organizes
asks	presents
behaves	processes
chooses	reflects
communicates	reshapes
considers	revises
creates	selects
devises	shares
demonstrates	shows
discovers	solves
evaluates	supports
exhibits	uses
expresses	utilizes
identifies	
implements	
interprets	

Sample Performance Standards

The following performance standards were written to assist and inspire performance standards work. While many of the standards written here should be relevant to all disciplines, we encourage revision, adjustment, or elaboration where appropriate. It is important that the standards conform to the vision of the assignment (not the other way around).

Creative Thinking
- The student organizes and processes symbols, pictures, graphs, objects, or other information.
- The student uses imagination to combine ideas or information.
- The student reshapes connections to reveal new possibilities.

Problem Solving
- The student considers, evaluates, and chooses among alternatives.
- The student uses learning techniques to apply and adapt to new knowledge and skills.
- The student discovers a rule or principle and applies it when solving a problem.
- The student identifies problems and possible reasons for discrepancies.
- The student devises and implements a plan of action to solve a problem.
- The student evaluates and monitors progress as indicated by findings.
- The student revise his or her plan of action to solve a problem.

Participation Skills
- The student asks appropriate questions to further the understanding of the topic.
- The student interprets and responds to the presenter's verbal and nonverbal cues.
- The student demonstrates active listening skills through appropriate body language and the recording of key information.
- The student shows receptivity to new ideas and perspectives.
- The student demonstrates an ability to organize and maintain a class notebook.
- The student shares responsibility with others to complete a group task.
- The student exercises leadership skills by driving forward the group's discussion, distribution of tasks, meeting of requirements, and time management.
- The student allocates time effectively to complete the assigned task(s).

Mathematical Skills
- The student expresses mathematical concepts and ideas orally and in writing.
- The student demonstrates an ability to perform basic computations.
- The student utilizes basic numerical concepts in practical situations.
- The student makes reasonable estimates of arithmetic results without a calculator.
- The student appropriately chooses from a variety of mathematical techniques to solve practical problems.

Writing Skills
- The student communicates thoughts, ideas, and information in writing.
- The student discusses and evaluates relevant information in the culminating

assignment.

- The student's work reflects appropriate attention to grammar, spelling, capitalization, and punctuation.
- The student demonstrates that he or she has made revisions to the original assignment based on the teacher's comments.
- The student demonstrates fluency with assigned vocabulary terms.
- The student supports major concepts with relevant details and specifications.
- The student locates, understands, and interprets assigned reading materials.
- The student evaluates the accuracy and plausibility of a piece of writing.
- The student monitors, evaluates, and adjusts his or her performance based on self-reflection and/or audience feedback.

Technology

- The student applies his or her understanding of technological tools to help complete the assigned task.
- The student prevents, identifies, or solves problems with equipment, including computers and other technologies.

Speaking Skills

- The student demonstrates an understanding of audience through selection of vocabulary, diction, tone, and body language.
- The student understands and responds to listeners' comments and questions.
- The student creates an organizational framework for the speech so that the audience can follow his or her train of thought.

Personal Skills

- The student assesses his or her own knowledge, skills, and abilities accurately; sets well-defined and realistic personal goals; and monitors progress toward goal attainment.
- The student behaves ethically in the creation and production of all assigned work.
- The student shows respect for other members of the class and demonstrates openness to opposing or different perspectives.
- The student exhibits internalization of self-directed principles: sets standards to achieve quality work, accepts responsibility, and understands the consequences of his or her actions.
- The student understands and applies conflict resolution strategies.

Troubleshooting Performance Standard Problems

1. How do you set up numerical values so that the grades come out right?

Remember, it must be possible for students to earn a total of 100 points. After you write your performance standards for a given assessment (usually between 4 and 10), select a number in the B range for standard so that you can add points in whole number increments.

Example:	5 standards, standard = 85;	check plus = +3
		check minus = −3
	8 standards, standard = 86;	check plus = +2
		check minus = −2
	9 standards, standard = 82;	check plus = +2
		check minus = −2

2. Why do you use checks, check pluses, and check minuses?

This system creates a very user-friendly scoring system. The pluses and minuses provide clear indicators to the students that they have fallen above or below standard. The concreteness of this concept communicates to them what areas they are doing well in and where they need to continue to make improvements.

3. I find that I am reluctant to give a student a zero. How often should I be using it?

The reluctance about using a zero stems from the harsh point penalty (10 point deduction). Zeros are an indication that the student has not made a sincere effort to address the performance standard in his or her work (whether the student forgot or deliberately chose not to include that requirement). The reason it is necessary to use zero in these situations is to keep the students focused on all requirements/values in the assignment and to keep the grades "honest"—that students who do not address the performance standard do not receive the same amount of points off their grades as students who try to meet the standard but fail to do so.

4. What happens if the performance standards do not fit my grading concerns?

If, after you distribute the performance standards to your students, you find that one of your standards is not working (either you are not sure what value you were trying to articulate or you are just not using it when scoring student work), you should not hold any students accountable to the standard. Remember, the standards are a contract you make with your students, and it is not fair to them to alter any standards after they have received them. Immediately change the standard the next time so that the original value is clearer or more relevant.

5. Can I reuse performance standards on different assignments?

Absolutely. In fact, many students find it reassuring to see certain standards used again because they already have a clear understanding of what is expected from them in that area. It is always a good idea, though, to double-check for small revisions to existing standards (e.g., continuing to clarify language, making a minor change to emphasize relevance to this assessment).

6. When should I hand out performance standards to the students?

We always distribute them with the assessment directions. In other words, as soon as you can after they receive the assessment—they really reinforce your directions/expectations.

7. Am I shortchanging the students by not writing more comments?

No! Even though you may be writing fewer comments, the comments that you do write are actually more helpful. By reacting to a specific standard, your comments will more concretely address the strengths or weaknesses of the particular work. They also will provide a better vehicle for communication between student and teacher in discussing grades and revising work.

Sample Student Assessment: Sustaining the City on the Hill

Essential Question
Are we in it for the money?

Directions:
This oral exam is designed to have students demonstrate the skills they have developed over the marking period, specifically performance arts, group collaboration, and making interdisciplinary connections. Each student in the group will select two of the following six decades:

1940s	1960s	1980s
1950s	1970s	1990s

The purpose of the oral presentation is to address the essential question for each decade by discussing two core values that seem to motivate people's behavior. This discussion must be supported *both by historical information and music lyrics from the time period*. These supplementary materials can be found through research time in the library media center (LMC). Because there is so much information and music for each decade, it is your responsibility to select two areas to focus on in more detail. The only written component of the exam is the creation of an outline for each decade to help the audience follow the speech. The outline should include the organizational framework of the decade presentation as well as the excerpts from the lyrics that will be included in the presentation.

Sample Outline Structure:
SUSTAINING THE CITY ON THE HILL IN THE **1930's**

Value #1
It is the government's responsibility to help people when they can no longer help themselves.

Outline
I. High unemployment rates made it difficult for Americans to take care of themselves.
    A. By the end of 1930, about 6 or 7 million workers in the United States were jobless. 100,000 Americans were being laid off each week.
    B. By 1932, nearly 13 million people were unemployed.

> *Excerpt from "Brother, Can You Spare a Dime?"*
> They used to tell me I was building a dream,
> And so I followed the mob
> When there was earth to plough or guns to bear
> I was always there right there on the job.
>
> They used to tell me I was building a dream
> With peace and glory ahead
> Why should I be standing in line
> Just waiting for bread?

II. People elected FDR in 1932 because of his promises that the government could do
   more to help the people.
   A. First 100 days in office
   B. Economic shift from laissez-faire to welfare state

Value #2
(same format as above)

Sample Student Outline: 1980's

Value #1
It was the government's job to restore values to society.
Outline
I. Ronald Reagan
    A. Background
        1. Began as governor of California and provided a tax rebate of over $6 billion to Californians.
        2. Tried to win presidential election of 1976
        3. Won presidential election of 1980
    B. Reaganomics
        1. Reduced taxes and reduced government spending
        2. People spent their extra money and expanded the economy
        3. Was passed as the Tax Act of 1981

Excerpt from "Heal the World" by Michael Jackson
And the dream we were conceived in
Will reveal a joyful face
And the world we once believed in
Will shine again in grace
Then why do we keep strangling life
Would this earth, crucify its soul
Though it's plain to see
This world is heavenly
Be God's glow

Value #2
Privacy was no longer necessary.
Outline
I. Everything was being pumped into the house.
    A. MTV launched
        1. First 100%-commercial station; every music video was advertising for someone
        2. Stores more convenient
            a. Wal-Mart
            b. K-Mart
        3. Computers
            a. IBM was releasing its first consumer computer
            b. Computer viruses were already making appearances

Excerpt from "Mr. Roboto" by Styx
I've got a secret I've been hiding under my skin
My heart is human, my blood is boiling, my brain IBM.
So if you see me acting strangely, don't be surprised
I'm just a man who needed someone, and somewhere to hide
To keep me alive—just keep me alive
Somewhere to hide to keep me alive

Performance Standards for Oral Exam

Standard is set at an 84. A check plus = +2, a check minus = −2. A zero (−10) will be given if the student does not make a good faith attempt to meet standard.

√   1. The students present the required number of decades (four or six depending on group size).

NOTE: You cannot exceed standard here.

All 6 decades were presented (three-person group).

√   2. The students use class and library time appropriately to work on the exam.

While we were really impressed with Dave's level of focus, Jane and John occasionally needed some prompting to stay on task.

√   3. The students present two core values for each decade to represent historical, political, social, and/or economic trends.

Values articulated on 1960s outline are the most clear, but on most of the other outlines your language needs to be revised to distinguish values from facts.

√+   4. The students develop a historical framework to support the significance of the value and the legitimacy of their interpretation.

Very good overview of a range of topics.

√   5. The students refer to specific dates, events, and people to demonstrate their research.

There are some interesting examples, but you could have developed topics more consistently throughout the presentation.

√+   6. The students deliver excerpts from music of the time period to enhance audience understanding and appreciation of each decade.

Best musical selections by far! The creation of the CD was a wonderful additional touch and made your musical clips seamless.

√+   7. The students offer an interpretation of the lyrics to show how they relate to the values and the history of the decade.

All three of you did an extraordinary job linking the music back to the values of both of her decades. Interesting to hear your interpretation of the music.

__√__   8. The students make a connection with the audience through the use of eye
             contact, volume, energy level, and voice inflection.

While none of you enjoy making oral presentations, you really have made some signifi-cant growth here. Continue to work on the eye contact with the audience. Jane, watch your speaking pace (a little too fast still).

__√–__   9. The students demonstrate their professionalism in the production of
             the outline and through proofreading and attention to layout.

Should have followed a more unified format among the three of you (font style, headings, etc.)

Name: <u>Jane Doe, John Smith, Dave Simpson</u>   Grade: <u>88</u>

Calculation Method: Standard = 84 (eight performance standards, check plus = +2,
             check minus = −2).
NOTE: There are only eight performance standards used in this calculation because on standard #1 students cannot exceed standard. Remember, only use the number of standards necessary in order for it to be possible for students to earn 100.

Grade = 5 checks, 3 check pluses, 1 check minus
84 . . . 84 + (3 × 2) = 90 . . . 90 − (1 × 2) = 88.
GRADE: 88

References

Darling-Hammond, Linda. (1993a). Reframing the School Reform Agenda. *Phi Delta Kappan, 74,* 753–761.

Darling-Hammond, Linda. (1993b). *The Right to Learn: A Blueprint for Creating Schools That Work.* San Francisco: Jossey-Bass.

Darling-Hammond, Linda, Jacqueline Ancess, & Beverly Falk. (1995). *Authentic Assessment in the Classroom.* New York: Teachers College Press.

Eliade, Mircea. (1954). *The Myth of the Eternal Return.* Princeton, NJ: Princeton University Press.

Glasser, William. (1986). *Control Theory in the Classroom.* New York: Harper & Row.

Glasser, William. (1992). *The Quality School Teacher.* New York: HarperCollins.

Hansche, Linda. (1998). *Handbook for the Development of Performance Standards.* Washington, DC: U.S. Department of Education and the Council of Chief State School Officers.

Kearns, David T., & Denis P. Doyle. (1988). *Winning the Brain Race.* San Francisco: Institute for Contemporary Studies.

Kobrin, David. (1992). *In There with the Kids.* Boston: Houghton Mifflin.

Mitchell, Ruth, Marilyn Willis, & the Chicago Teachers Union Quest Center. (1995). *Learning in Overdrive: Designing Curriculum, Instruction, and Assessment from Standards.* Golden, CO: North American Press.

Sizer, Theodore R. (1984). *Horace's Compromise.* Boston: Houghton Mifflin.

Sizer, Theodore R. (1986). Rebuilding: First Steps by the Coalition of Essential Schools. *Phi Delta Kappan, 68,* 38–42.

Sizer, Theodore R. (1992). *Horace's School.* Boston: Houghton Mifflin.

Tucker, Marc S., & Judy B. Codding. (1998). *Standards for Our Schools.* San Francisco: Jossey-Bass.

Wasley, Patricia A. (1994). *Stirring the Chalkdust: Tales of Teachers Changing Classroom Practices.* New York: Teachers College Press.

Wasley, Patricia A., Robert L. Hampel, & Richard W. Clark. (1997). *Kids and School Reform.* San Francisco: Jossey-Bass.

Wiggins, Grant, & Jay McTighe. (1998). *Understanding by Design.* Alexandria, VA: Association for Supervision and Curriculum Development.

Index

About the Authors

Allison Zmuda received her B.A. from Yale University and her M.A.L.S. from Wesleyan University, both in American Studies. She has spent all 7 years of her teaching career as a social studies teacher in Newtown, Connecticut. Allison also has launched her own educational consulting business to provide professional development services for teachers. She and her husband live in Woodbury, Connecticut.

Mary Tomaino has degrees in English from Western and Southern Connecticut State Universities. She taught English and American Studies in Newtown, Connecticut, for 32 years, before retiring to write, read books she did not assign, and spend time with family. She and her family live in Danbury, Connecticut.